Unicornia Unveiled

Dismantling DEI, the Decline of Men, and Questioning
Climate Orthodoxy

Bob Rosic

DEFIANCE PRESS & PUBLISHING, LLC

DEFIANCE PRESS
& PUBLISHING

Unicornia Unveiled: Dismantling DEI, the Decline of Men, and Questioning Climate Orthodoxy
By Robert Rosic
© 2025 All rights reserved.

This is a work of fiction. Names, characters, businesses, places, events, and incidents are either the products of the author's imagination or used in a fictitious manner. Any resemblance to actual persons, living or dead, or actual events is purely coincidental

Published by:
Defiance Press & Publishing, LLC
www.defiancepress.com

ISBN:
eBook: 978-1-966625-04-9
Paperback: 978-1-966625-05-6
Printed in the United States of America

For permission requests or inquiries, contact Defiance Press & Publishing at: publishing@defiancepress.com

Contents

PROLOGUE: A BEACON FROM UNICORNIA

In a world where the fabric of reality is woven with threads of whimsy and satire, Unicornia emerges not just as a fictional realm but as a beacon of critique against the backdrop of the West's cultural and societal shifts. This prologue serves as an entryway, not just into a fantastical narrative, but into a reflective journey through the ideologies and movements that shape our contemporary existence.

The concept of Diversity, Equity, and Inclusion (DEI) has, in its application, become a contentious force, reshaping institutions and societal norms. While the ideals behind DEI are ostensibly noble, aiming to foster equality and inclusivity, its execution often leads to a paradoxical outcome where diversity of thought is suppressed, and equity is pursued at the expense of meritocracy. This book does not shy away from discussing these contradictions, challenging the reader to consider how DEI has inadvertently contributed to the decline of Western values that once championed individual freedoms and equality of opportunity.

Parallel to the rise of DEI, there's a noticeable shift in the portrayal and treatment of men in Western culture. Once seen as stalwarts of society, there's now a narrative that paints them as either oppressors or obsolete, a narrative this book seeks to dissect. By exploring the challenges men face today—ranging from educational disparities to societal expectations—we aim to foster a dialogue on how to recalibrate the scales to ensure a balanced approach to gender issues, one that does not diminish one gender to elevate another.

Climate alarmism, another cornerstone of contemporary Western discourse, often overshadows a more nuanced understanding of environmental issues. While the global warming discussion is important, the book argues for a departure from the hysteria that often characterizes this debate. It calls for a re-evaluation of the data, the economics, and the proposed solutions, advocating for a more rational, science-driven approach over the emotional appeals that dominate public discourse.

Unicornia, in its essence, is not merely a narrative of fantasy but a satirical commentary on these very issues. Created as a realm where the absurdities of our current socio-political climate are taken to their logical extremes, it serves as a wake-up call. It's a place where the ideas of DEI, the downfall of men, and climate orthodoxy are not just discussed but lived out in ways that highlight their potential pitfalls. Through humor, Unicornia invites us to laugh, but also to think critically about the path we're on.

This book, through the lens of Unicornia, aims to dismantle certain ideologies not out of malice, but out of a profound concern for the future of Western civilization. It argues that freedom of thought, the cornerstone of democracy, is under threat from these very movements that claim to champion equality and justice. By discussing these topics openly, we seek to ignite a conversation that might seem controversial but is necessary for the health of our society.

The creation of Unicornia, therefore, is not simply an act of storytelling but an act of rebellion. It's a rebellion against the status quo that refuses to question itself, against the dogmas that demand adherence without scrutiny. By presenting a world where these ideas are taken to their extremes, the book not only entertains but educates, prompting readers to reconsider the narratives they've accepted as truth.

As we embark on this journey through Unicornia, let us remember that the purpose is not to demean or belittle but to provoke thought and encourage debate. The book does not claim to have all the answers but seeks to pose questions that many might find uncomfortable. It's a call to arms for those who value freedom, rationality, and the pursuit of truth over comfort and conformity.

In this book, we confront some of the most pervasive and insidious trends that are contributing to the decline of Western society. Chief among these are the ideologies surrounding Diversity, Equity, and Inclusion (DEI), the shifting cultural perceptions and treatment of men, and the dogmatic adherence to Climate Orthodoxy. Each of these elements, while perhaps rooted in noble intentions, has morphed into a vehicle for driving deep divisions and fostering resentment within our communities.

DEI, as it is currently implemented, often prioritizes quotas over merit and uniformity over genuine diversity of thought, leading to environments where innovation and freedom of expression are stifled. Similarly, the modern narrative surrounding masculinity has seen men increasingly portrayed in negative lights, undermining their roles within families and society, and contributing to a destabilizing shift in social dynamics. Meanwhile, Climate Orthodoxy has been weaponized to justify sweeping economic and social policies that lack sufficient scientific rigor or debate, placing immense strain on our economic structures and personal freedoms.

It is imperative that we address these issues decisively and with open dialogue. The future of Western civilization depends on our ability to challenge these destructive doctrines and replace them with principles that truly foster an inclusive, fair, and thriving society. We must strive for solutions that respect individual merits, honor our varied roles in society, and encourage a balanced approach to global challenges. The time to act is now—before the foundations of our culture are irreparably damaged.

In the kaleidoscopic world of Unicornia, the boundaries of reality blur and fantasy takes center stage. It is a realm constructed by the creative and fervent minds of teenage social justice warriors, where absurdity reigns supreme and the ordinary is left far behind. Beneath its seemingly whimsical façade, Unicornia unveils a profound commentary, serving as a metaphorical mirror to the Western world's evolving sociopolitical landscape. It delves into the damaging impacts DEI initiatives and explores the downfall of men in Western culture, and the excessive political correctness that permeates Western Culture. Unicornia is the ultimate matriarchy and while it is a fantasy land, we are being propelled to this whimsical land.

Unicornia, with its metaphorical unicorns and ever-smiling suns, is not merely a stage for satirical conjectures; it is a stage upon which the erosion of fundamental democratic values is laid bare. The gradual decline of freedom and liberty, once considered the bedrock of Western civilizations, is unveiled amidst the colorful pastures and rainbow skies of this fantastical land. Through humor and gravity, Unicornia serves as a mirror to our current reality, where the principles of democracy and free speech are under siege, echoing the concerns of our forebearers.

This imaginative journey goes beyond the realm of entertainment; it is a clarion call to action. A wake-up call to awaken from complacency and ignite the flame of liberty before it is extinguished by the encroaching winds of authoritarianism. Unicornia challenges us to reevaluate the value of freedom, to recognize its significance, and to envision a future where it is not merely protected but passionately championed.

However, in this pursuit, harnessing the power of marketing becomes paramount. Unicornia's intricate dance of ideas teaches us that the discourse surrounding liberty can be elevated through a clever fusion of wit, wisdom, and words. By doing so, we can make the cause of freedom an irresistible beacon for those who find themselves in the shadows of oppression. Unicornia is a testament to the importance of advocating for freedom in a way that resonates, stimulates dialogue, and inspires a collective desire to safeguard our cherished liberties.

In essence, Unicornia serves as a whimsical yet poignant reminder of the precarious state of the Western world, where contradictions abound and authoritarian threats loom. It invites us to traverse a landscape where laughter and solemn reflection intertwine, urging us to reassess our position, question the erosion of our values, and commit ourselves anew to upholding the ideals that have long defined the essence of Western civilization.

After exploring Unicornia, this book, we will critically examine the influence of DEI practices that require reconsideration and, ultimately, dismantling. Our discussion will culminate in a compelling call to action, offering clear, practical steps to move away from these prevailing illusions towards a more stable and promising future. In addition, our journey will delve into the significant challenges that men face in contemporary society, advocating for an educational system that prioritizes true intellectual growth over ideological indoctrination.

Equally crucial is our exploration of the climate dogma that pervades current discourse. This book challenges the religious fervor of the environmental movement, advocating for a much-needed conversation about the scientific, economic, and social realities often ignored in climate activism. By questioning the unchallenged assumptions and the alarmist rhetoric that dominate the field, we aim to foster a more informed, rational dialogue that respects both the complexity of the climate issue.

Now, before we delve deeper into the satirical insights of Unicornia, it is essential to take a brief detour into the real world, a narrative that underscores my roots and connection to the complexities of our messy reality. This connection provides a vital anchor to the fantastical voyage through Unicornia, making it all the more relevant and thought-provoking.

A Drummer's Tale of Hair Metal, Grit, and an Unforgettable Small-Town Showdown

Before we dive into this melodrama, let me make one thing abundantly clear. Some of you may misinterpret this work as an endorsement of the far right or presume that I've nestled comfortably in their ranks. The mere suggestion of such a notion is as preposterous as a fish on a bicycle, but for the sake of clarity, let me share a little tale to dispel any lingering doubt.

Once upon a time in the dog days of summer of 1989, I got a call from a friend, the kind of call that could only spell adventure—or disaster. A travelling club band on a North American tour needed a temporary drummer, and the gig was just one week away. My inner Mick Tucker leapt at the chance. For those who might be scratching their heads, Mick Tucker is my favorite rock drummer of all time. I've always wanted to give him a nod in my writings, so consider this my subtle shout-out. It was about time!

I rang up the bar owner who directed me to the band's singer. As it turned out, the set list was full of songs I knew, and they were a hair metal band—a fact that carried two conditions: one, I had to be fit (check) and two, I had to be comfortable in makeup (untested, but willing). I mean, who could resist a little bit of Bowie-esque sparkle?

We set the stage for our inaugural encounter at a downtown Hamilton coffee shop, a nonpartisan terrain where one would typically anticipate a cordial exchange of small talk, not the ebb and flow of a glitzy rock band's exploits. As they sauntered in, each member of the ensemble reminded me of a parade of svelte flamingos, resplendent in their spandex plumage, their collective weight probably less than that of my drum kit.

As for me, I cut a figure more akin to a gridiron maven than an 80s hair band rock drummer. But let's be clear: when it came to hair, I was more than qualified. With locks cascading halfway down my back, I was practically audition-ready from the hair perspective alone! Nevertheless, I arrived wearing a blazer, presenting a somewhat pristine veneer of formality. Yet, as the conversation progressed, a budding sense of camaraderie began to form. Feeling the warmth of this newfound rapport, I decided it was time to shake things up a bit. Off came the blazer, revealing a simple, yet snug t-shirt underneath, and my glorious mane took center stage. Who said hair wasn't an instrument?

A ripple of surprise and acknowledgment ran through the band at this unexpected change. One of them, a fellow Miami Dolphins enthusiast, studied me with a calculating eye, as if sizing up a promising quarterback. He looked from my footwear, up to my now-revealed attire, finally meeting my gaze, a smirk tugging at the corner of his lips.

His words punctuated the moment, "You know, your height and physique are strikingly similar to Mark Clayton's," he quipped, invoking the name of the Dolphins' legendary wide receiver. His comment carried a note of jest, yet it was imbued with a certain degree of sincerity.

I couldn't help but feel a bit flattered by the unexpected comparison to one of my favourite receivers at the time, even as he quickly appended his remark with, "Minus the six-pack, of course!" His words incited a round of shared laughter, an implicit understanding of camaraderie forming amongst us. The playful banter, just like the rhythm of a song, was flowing freely, setting the stage for the incredible journey we were about to undertake.

Truth be told, I had spent a fair share of my youth at the wide receiver position, catching passes and dodging tackles. Friends and teammates often compared my style of play to Clayton's - we were of a similar height, and it seemed, shared a knack for the dramatic catch. But on this day, it was less about my skills on the football field and more about fitting into the hair metal scene.

The band's lead singer, peering at me over his sunglasses, declared my look was "too Glass Tiger and not enough Warrant." Apparently, my blazer, t-shirt-and-jeans ensemble was not quite the spandex spectacle they were hoping for. Despite my physique being more 'Miami Dolphins wide receiver,' it seemed that I needed to channel more hair metal vibes to truly gel with the band.

I was an anomaly, a touch too "Glass Tiger" for their 'Cherry Pie'-esque preferences. But, with the gig's countdown ticking relentlessly, they swallowed their apprehension and decided to give 'beefy' old me a shot.

Rehearsals ensued and the music flowed, albeit with the occasional speed bump—the sort you'd expect when you're rehearsing with a new drummer on such short notice. Post-practice, I was cordially invited to an after-party that was scheduled to follow our second show.

On the day of the show, the band's lead singer turned make-up artist and began applying a heavy dose of glamour to my face. As I peered at my reflection, I was met with the sight of me wearing make-up. I looked like a cross between a glam rock drummer and a Canadian Football League wide receiver after a night of heavy partying. Suddenly, I could comprehend their initial apprehension about my appearance during our meet and greet. The incongruity was undeniable, yet oddly enough, it worked. I guess in the wild world of hair metal rock, stranger things have happened.

With my Rocky Horror Picture Show-like transformation complete, my focus shifted to the upcoming gigs and the impending, undoubtedly wild after-party. Little did I know, the wheels of my brief stint in the hair metal world were about to turn in the most unexpected of directions.

Our first show in Hamilton was like a neon lit dream, the crowd cheering and clapping along to the music. And let's be real here, while my bandmates were rocking the spandex like they were born in it, I was clad in a blazer and jeans, a wardrobe choice dictated by the wide receiver-like physique. If anyone in that crowd was expecting a glam band version of the NFL, I certainly didn't disappoint!

The second gig was like watching a comedy of errors unfold in the dim lighting of a small-town tavern. Picture this: a gaggle of befuddled squirrels suddenly thrust into a disco. The local patrons mirrored them, their expressions juggling bewilderment, mild panic, and a sprinkling of "What on earth did I just walk into?" And let's be real - amidst this quirky, spandex-wearing ensemble, here I stood in my blazer, jeans, and on-point makeup, looking as if I'd accidentally crash-landed from a corporate boardroom. To say I stood out would be an understatement. With every strum and beat, it was abundantly clear – their usual pint night had taken quite the turn.

Boos echoed off the bar walls like a bad sitcom laugh track. Uncomfortable doesn't quite cut it, but we powered through, packed up, and skedaddled out of there as quickly as we could.

Here's where the story takes a turn. As we were loading the gear, nature called, and I stepped away for a few minutes. By the time I came back, two bald-headed troublemakers were harassing the band, pushing them around and spewing insults. It was a scene straight out of a bad 80s movie, and not one of the fun ones with a rocking soundtrack. The bandmates were shocked into inaction, staring at their tormentors like deer caught in the headlights.

Oh, how I wish I could tell you that I channeled my inner John Wick at this moment, that I sprang into action with a cool head and a killer instinct, dispatching the pair of thugs with a flurry of precision punches. That I stood victorious over them, the triumphant hero, the band cheering in the background... But, in reality, it was a two-on-one situation, and I knew I was in serious trouble. As much as I'd like to paint myself as a stoic hero, reality tends to be messier. But let's get back to the story.

A little background: growing up as part of one of the few Slavic families in a tough neighborhood, I'd become rather adept at delivering a punch or two. Without hesitating, I gave one skinhead a firm shove and offered his friend a swift left hook. My bandmates, on the other hand, looked like they'd been training for a duel with an ornery pillow rather than these bruisers.

Having just taken on two intimidating figures, my adrenaline was already coursing at full speed. With every aching muscle and heightened breath, I felt the weight of the situation. The roar of an engine immediately triggered horrifying visions in my mind: of being pummeled by not two, but three assailants, and waking up in a cold, sterile hospital room. A guy on a motorcycle, seemingly plucked straight from my darkest nightmares — inked from head to toe and draped in imposing leather — stormed onto the scene. My heart raced as panic took hold, bracing myself for the imminent onslaught. But, in a twist I hadn't seen coming, this fierce-looking new arrival parked himself squarely beside me. With a fearless sneer, he addressed the skinheads: "Okay boys, let's do this two on two, a fair fight." The skinheads, suddenly realizing their numbers no longer guaranteed dominance, hesitated momentarily. Their false bravado quickly faded, and they turned tail, scurrying away in their typical cowardly fashion.

After the dust settled, we found ourselves chatting with our leather-clad savior, the roar of the motorcycle still lingering in the air. The behavior of the bar crowd inevitably became the topic of conversation. With a shake of his head and a gesture towards the bar, he made it clear: "Those skinheads and this bar—they don't represent the heart of this community." Offering an apologetic look, he added, "Sorry you had to see that side tonight." It was a poignant reminder that, even in the most unexpected places, there are always individuals who stand for what's right. This motorcycle-riding guardian angel was one such beacon amidst the chaos.

We bid our farewells to our leather clad helper, and I handed the band one piece of advice, "In places like this, always hire security."

As for the afterparty, well, that's a tale in itself. Let's just say that it could easily have served as the plot for an R-rated movie, a wild concoction of hair-spray-infused rock 'n' roll energy, questionable fashion choices, and so much spandex that it was practically a character in itself. To keep things somewhat within the realm of the PG-13, I'll spare you the vivid details. But rest assured, it was an evening as unforgettable as the eyeshadow that refused to wash off my face for the next few days. Yes, the 80s were a time to be alive, folks

Now, for those who might not be familiar with the term, these 'skinheads' were what we'd nowadays likely label as the far-right. Oh, the sweet irony! Picture it now: me, joining the very group I spent my younger years tangling with, dodging punches and slurs alike! You might as well ask a vegan to endorse a steakhouse. Simply preposterous.

In my youth, while my altercations with the far-right were infrequent, when they did occur, they were remarkably nasty. I tangled with these chaps a handful of times, and trust me, none of those encounters culminated in us harmonizing to 'Kumbaya' around a campfire. Now, picture me, of all people, being misidentified as one of their rank and file. It feels as though I've been thrust into a surreal alternate universe where up is down, black is white, and I've inexplicably acquired a taste for conspiracy theories and intolerance.

Indeed, the world has its baffling twists and turns. Here I stand, a bastion of rationality, and yet I'm accused of siding with the very forces I abhor. It's like being caught in the most egregious case of mistaken identity. Let me make this abundantly clear: no matter the label or guise, the repugnant stench of bigotry and prejudice is unmistakable. And believe me, there isn't a fragrance in existence potent enough to cloak such a noxious cloud.

And now, dear reader, having banished any notions of me being a far-right mouthpiece to the land of spandex and hair metal, it's time to dive headfirst into the frothy waters of absurdity.

In the modern 21st century, our lives have transcended the mundane and ventured into the realm of the utterly absurd. Some would argue it's humor; others might think of it as a tragicomedy. But no matter how you slice it, one thing is certain: it's definitely not what the Enlightenment philosophers had in mind.

This is satire. This is about highlighting the hilarity in our current predicaments and showing that sometimes, the best way to deal with the overwhelming is to laugh at it, loudly and unapologetically.

My dream had always been clearly etched in my mind's canvas: sipping coffee in quaint cafes, reflecting on the ebb and flow of life; the sheer exhilaration of an occasional ball hockey game, and perhaps even some spirited flag football under the evening sky. When the dusk settled, I would find solace in the pages of a captivating book, spending time with close family and embracing the comforting hum of my introverted existence. In this vision, I'd continue dedicating my hours to my psychology practice, assisting those disadvantaged souls in securing the disability benefits they rightly deserved. Whenever inspiration struck, I'd pen down my thoughts or craft melodies, recording songs that whispered tales of my experiences. Yet, life, with its inherent unpredictability, always tested the horizons of my dreams. The charming dance of Unicornia amid the ever-growing peculiarities of this realm called out. Rather than blending into the shadows, destiny seemed to push me center stage, urging me to observe, maybe even narrate, the unfolding drama of our era.

So, dear reader, while Mars might seem like an appealing alternative when faced with our world's strange and sometimes terrifying realities, let's first journey through Unicornia. Let's pull back the curtain on the comedic chaos and, together, dive headfirst into the absurdities that make our world both maddening and magical.

A Journey to Unicornia

Dear reader, brace yourself to traverse the vibrant, holographic rainbow bridge into a realm bound not by tiresome rationality, but drenched in the dazzling glow of wokeness: Unicornia.

This is a place where the sturdy grain of common sense is meticulously pulverized into the iridescent pixie dust of unabashed optimism, where intellectual depth is as shallow as a unicorn's wading pool, where the world is observed not through the clear glass of objectivity, but through the mesmerizing swirl of a social justice kaleidoscope.

Welcome to the ultimate dream of the social justice warrior, a land of vibrant rainbows and sparkling safe spaces. A land where each opinion, no matter how fanciful or whimsical, is held aloft like a sacred relic. A land where disagreement is as mythical as the winged creatures that dot its glittering skyline.

Yes, a world conjured up by the boundless imagination of an impressionable pre-teen, fueled by an unending diet of fantastical fables, shimmering glitter, and an ardent dismissal of mundane reality, has finally manifested itself as the ideal society.

In Unicornia, concepts such as meritocracy, free speech, and even biology are as extinct as the dinosaurs. They are now mere relics of a bygone era, a time before the great enlightenment dawned. In their stead, a collective of virtue signaling lords, lady knights of cancel culture, and jesters of juvenile ideas rule the roost.

Dawn in Unicornia

Every morning in Unicornia starts not with the crowing of roosters or the dawning of the sun, but with the punctual tolling of the Privilege Clock, nestled at the heart of the city square. But this isn't your average timekeeping device; oh no, it's a grand monument forged from recycled glass bottles and colored with organic, vegan paint. It's a visual spectacle, a powerful symbol of Unicornia's commitment to environmental righteousness.

The true importance of this clock lies not in its aesthetics but in the message, it chimes each dawn. As the sky blushes pink, a mere coincidence and not a microaggression towards any particular color, mind you, the clock tolls. The sound is neither harsh nor grating but a melodious symphony composed by the renowned Maestro of Microaggressions, whose very name sends shivers down the politically correct spine of Unicornia.

Now here's where the genius kicks in: as the chime travels across the kaleidoscopic landscape, slipping through glittering towers, breezing past rainbow sidewalks, it magically personalizes itself to each Unicornian, thanks to the groundbreaking technology developed by the Department of Wokeness. It's a brilliant feat, ensuring that the chimes transform into a customized holographic display at each home, accurately reflecting one's unique privilege score.

This individualized morning call serves as a reminder of the societal debt every Unicornian owes, a melodious reckoning of privilege points that must be acknowledged before breakfast is even considered. And heaven forbid one eats breakfast without acknowledging privilege! The last person who tried that was assigned to a week-long seminar on "Empathetic Chewing."

You see, in Unicornia, worth isn't quantified by something as archaic as skill, ambition, or accomplishments. No, no. Instead, the systemic guilt calculator determines one's standing in society. This calculator uses algorithms so complex that even the Unicornian mathematicians who created it often get lost in its maze, only to emerge days later mumbling about intersectionality and gluten-free pie charts.

As the clock tolls fade, each Unicornian begins their day by ritually acknowledging their privilege, with some even hosting brunches to competitively out-acknowledge each other. It's a deeply personal moment, a sacred daily practice that's as integral to the Unicornian lifestyle as glitter, rainbows, and well, unicorns.

The Privilege Clock doesn't just dictate the start of each day; it sets the rhythm of Unicornian existence. This isn't a dystopian alarm meant to impose guilt; it's an emblem of enlightenment, a call to perpetual self-awareness, and a daily reminder that in the land of Unicornia, the privilege of a few must always be accounted for, and the societal debt repaid, one melodious, personalized toll at a time.

Possessions and Progress in Unicornia

Unicornia, a land of eternal rainbows and shared spaces, where ownership is considered a taboo, and possessions, a vestige of the crude past, have gracefully transitioned to communal sharing.

In the avant-garde utopia of Unicornia, the antiquated notion of "personal property" is as outmoded as a VHS tape. Money? Oh, that crinkly relic! We've cast it aside in the same way one would discard last season's unicorn horn design.

Here, everyone's abode is a mirror image of the next. No need for those gauche "MTV Cribs" episodes or Instagram home tours. Why, you ask? Because everyone's living room has the same gleaming (and perfectly ergonomic) unicorn-shaped couch, the identical celestial-themed drapery, and the same cutting-edge sound system that, interestingly, only plays harp renditions of pop songs.

And the sense of equity doesn't stop at your doorstep. Open your neighbor's cupboard, and you'll find the exact number of crystal goblets, all imprinted with the official Unicornia seal. Peek into their wardrobe, and you'll see the same seven outfits for each day of the week. It's like "Groundhog Day," but with fashion!

Why such uniformity? Because in Unicornia, we've cracked the code. Envy, competition, the rat race of consumerism... all extinguished. We've achieved the epitome of community spirit! Here, you won't feel superior with a bigger chandelier or inferior with a smaller TV. Because guess what? They're all the same size!

Now, if you're pondering about individuality or personal expression, worry not! You can always choose the color of your toothbrush... as long as it's one of the fifty shades of pastel.

And, these aren't your traditional homes, oh no, Unicornians dwell in futuristic 'Social Pods.' These self-sustaining, eco-friendly housing units dot the cityscape, each one no larger than the space strictly necessary to maintain a minimalist existence. After all, excessive living space is a waste, isn't it? Everything inside these pods is uniform and utility-focused, from the recyclable clothing to the nutritious algae-based food. Even the in-pod entertainment is carefully curated by the Department of Wokeness, offering a balanced diet of thoughtfully engineered shows promoting societal harmony and awareness.

The suburbs, once teeming with homes and families, now serve as protected lands, grand reserves for Mother Nature's children to reclaim. Highways have turned into migratory paths, backyard pools into watering holes, and parks into evergreen forests. The serenity of the suburbs is only interrupted by the gentle rustle of the wind, the occasional hoot of an owl, or the stealthy prowl of a fox. The land where barbecues and neighborhood parties once took place now echoes with the sounds of undisturbed nature.

When it comes to transportation, the once gleaming personal vehicles are replaced with communal Eco-Pods, driverless vehicles running on renewable energy that whir silently across the rainbow boulevards. Personal transportation is now viewed as an indulgent practice of the past. Instead, public transit is considered a collective act of social responsibility.

And then, there's travel. In Unicornia, the right to explore the world is a privilege accorded only to the leaders, the enlightened ones chosen to guide society. They travel on diplomatic missions or to engage in vital cultural exchanges, collecting global wisdom to infuse back into the heart of Unicornia. For the everyday citizen, world travel is a once-in-five-years treat, a controlled measure to maintain environmental sustainability.

You see, in Unicornia, travel is no longer a leisure activity but an earned privilege. It's viewed as a sacred practice, a pilgrimage where Unicornians learn and bring back lessons to implement in their homeland. The excitement surrounding these journeys is palpable. After all, who needs to see the world regularly when you live in a utopia?

And so, in this perfect city-state, the shackles of ownership have been cast aside, and the restrictions of travel are embraced. Unicornians live not for themselves, but for the collective, in a world where progress isn't measured by personal acquisitions, but by the continual minimization of societal guilt and the protection of Mother Nature. In Unicornia, the grass grows free, the animals roam unrestricted, and the citizens exist in an enlightened state of shared minimalism, under the ever-watchful eyes of their wise leaders.

In the rainbow-colored land of Unicornia, traditional notions of wealth and want have been thoroughly reimagined. You see, here, residents don't clamor for gold or silver. Oh no, that's far too passé. Instead, they trade in 'virtue coins', a shimmering currency that's as much about moral worth as it is about purchasing power. The fascinating twist? The more coins you possess, the more you're gently nudged—nay, enthusiastically encouraged—to atone for the heinous crime of being "monetarily gifted". But, before you wrinkle your brow in sympathy for the 'poor', hold that thought. In Unicornia, they've banished such derogatory terms. There's no 'poverty' here, thank you very much. Citizens either bask in their 'financial opulence' or revel in their status as the 'economically diverse'. And in this land of equal dreams and equal whimsy, everyone sleeps soundly, wrapped in blankets of satirical bliss.

REMORSE AND RAINBOWS: THE RITES OF UNICORNIA

In the heart of Unicornia, where rainbows cascade from cotton candy clouds and dreams seem as tangible as the ground beneath your hooves, lies a peculiar tradition that defines the very essence of its inhabitants. On the calendar, marked with stars and sprinkled with pixie dust, is the most awaited day of all – the Day of Apologies.

The Day of Apologies isn't just any other celebration; it's a solemn rite of passage. From the oldest elder, whose mane has witnessed countless cycles of the shimmering northern lights, to the youngest foal, still glistening from the morning dew of birth, everyone congregates at the legendary Apology Stone. This isn't just any stone, mind you. It's said that the Apology Stone was chiseled from the tears of a thousand misunderstood unicorns and holds the power to absorb the collective regrets of the community.

It is rumored that the more heartfelt the apology, the more the Apology Stone glows, rewarding the sincerest of souls with a temporary halo. This halo isn't just a symbol of right-eousness but also gives the bearer the ability to see the world through a lens of extreme empathy for exactly one day.

Yet, the ceremony does not end there. After every unicorn has offered their remorseful murmurs to the Apology Stone, the entire assembly engages in a group hug. This hug, known as the Embrace of Empathy, is believed to charge Unicornia with an energy so positive that flowers bloom instantly and stars shoot across the daytime sky.

As the sun sets, painting the sky with hues that reflect the emotional roller-coaster of the day, Unicornians retire to their homes – made of recycled wishes, naturally – and reflect upon the lessons of the day. They drift into dreams, already eagerly anticipating next year's Day of Apologies, and the chance to once again cleanse their collective conscience.

The Sacred Sound of Silence & Watchful Ears of Order

In the gentle breezes of Unicornia, where the very elements pronounce their identities with grace, logic and fact are not the prime currencies of discourse. Here, sentiment reigns supreme. It's a reality where even the winds whisper their pronouns as they dance through the shimmering, glitter-strewn streets. The rainbows? They too have voices, demanding their right not to be touched, especially if they're having a day where they identify more as sunshowers.

Ah, and just as the harmonious winds gently caress the face, our beloved Patriarchy Patrol is ever-present, maintaining this melodious equilibrium. The mere whisper of unkindness, the faintest utterance of disagreement, and a fleet of eco-friendly vehicles with their iconic unicorn emblem swiftly make their appearance. The sirens? Oh, they don't blare; they hum harmoniously, reminding the citizens of the gentle caress of Mother Nature.

Should you dare to utter a slur or let slip a microaggression, the vehicles surround you, and the officers, with their soft-glowing badges, descend with purpose. They gently but firmly guide the perpetrator to one of the city's famed Speech Training Centers. The goal? To cleanse the mind and tongue of all hate, replacing it with sweet harmonious expressions that soothe the soul and nurture the spirit.

Now, when disputes do arise, and they are infrequent in this sea of sameness, there's no resorting to the harsh judgments of yesteryears. Instead, the ancient art of 'safe-space sparring' steps into the limelight. Two opposing parties gracefully share their feelings in a carefully designed sanctuary, where the ambiance is always set to "tranquil." There, whoever spins the most emotionally compelling narrative emerges the victor. There's no room for disagreement here; the ever-vigilant Patrol ensures it.

So, in Unicornia, words are not just sounds; they are symphonies of kindness, echoed and maintained under the watchful gaze of the Patriarchy Patrol. Here, the old adage rings true: if you have nothing nice to say, the Patrol will teach you how.

Equal Minds in Unicornia: The Leveling of Intellectual Landscapes

In the technicolor panorama of Unicornia, where equity isn't just a virtue but the very air one breathes, those towering IQ societies are seen as archaic remnants of a less enlightened time. In the meadows of Unicornia, where each blade of grass proudly boasts its own glittering hue, the idea of a 'high IQ' is as unsavory as the forbidden beef delicacy of ancient times.

How absurd, right, that in past eras, some were celebrated for their cognitive altitude, while others, in the grand dance of neural diversity, were left twirling in the shadows. It's particularly vexing to think that one could be applauded for the mere neural configuration of their mind. Surely, as we believe in Unicornia, intelligence, like sprinkles on our morning insect-toast, should be sprinkled evenly.

Did Einstein with his wild hair and wilder theories deserve all those accolades while others struggled with the basic intricacies of a children's puzzle? The audacity of such distinction! All those countless nights, immersed in profound contemplation, the insatiable thirst for knowledge, the endless sacrifices at the altar of discovery? Here in Unicornia, we have a more holistic approach – equal accolades for all, irrespective of their endeavors or depths of thought.

Our aim? To homogenize intellect. To spread knowledge as evenly as we spread almond-butter on our vegan crackers, regardless of one's affinity or appetite for such wisdom. A land where everyone feels like a genius, and no one ever experiences the slight sting of envy or inadequacy.

Picture a Unicornia where understanding quantum physics is as straightforward as following the dramatic twists of our national soap opera, "Unicorns & Unison." Envision the egalitarian conversations, where every spoken word is received with a nod and an "I know, right?", with nobody's brilliance eclipsing another.

Now, for the few who hark back to days of old, emphasizing the innovations birthed by extraordinary intellects or the necessity for adept minds in nuanced domains, we in Unicornia have a gentle response. Educate them, under the twinkling stars and with the soft hum of the Patriarchy Patrol's eco-friendly vehicles in the distance. Such souls, with their adherence to outdated logic, are but misaligned notes in our symphonic dream.

So, journey with us in Unicornia, the zenith of an intellectually harmonized realm!

LOUD WHISPERS OF SILENCE: THE UNSPOKEN PERFECTION OF UNICORNIA

Bid your farewell to that antiquated notion of freedom of speech and take a leap into the crystal-clear pools of unanimous agreement that permeate the shimmering plains of Unicornia. Here, dissent is as extinct as the sabre-toothed tiger and harmony is the heartbeat of the land.

In this futuristic haven, the Council of Universal Consensus, those benevolent guardians of harmony, have interwoven all human thought into a perfect tapestry of shared belief. Their tireless dedication to eliminate discord and disarray has made the need for free speech seem as outdated as the floppy disk.

Across this utopia, public spaces once plagued with soapbox speakers have been transformed into harmonious hubs of synchronized yoga, while universities, freed from the shackles of controversial speakers, now offer enriching courses such as "Advanced Nodding" and "Harmony Harmonics 101". Social media, a ubiquitous echo chamber, resonates with unified thoughts and beliefs. The only button, the 'like' button, automatically pressed, reflects this unanimity.

Art and Allegiance in Unicornia: The Tale of the Council of Art Equity

In the pastel shades of Unicornia, art and expression might seem boundless, yet their horizons are meticulously curated. The Council of Art Equity, or CAE as they're affectionately known, stands as the guardian of the collective heart and soul of the land. While some might say that the purpose of art is to challenge and provoke thought, in Unicornia, it serves a higher purpose - to cultivate unity, tranquility, and a perpetual echo of the state's utopian vision.

Each film that graces the silver screens of Unicornia cinemas is not merely entertainment; it's a celebration of the same dream: a world without conflict, full of rainbows and harmonious vibes. Every ending is a happy one, and every protagonist, irrespective of their journey, reaches the same epiphany about love, kindness, and the essence of Unicornian values.

Songs, too, have their rhythms and rhymes scrutinized for discordant sentiments. The melodies that waft from radios, shops, and homes are harmonious, almost hypnotic in their uniformity. Strolling through the boulevards of Unicornia, one hears the same tunes being hummed, whistled, and sung by its citizens. It's as if the entire nation dances to the same beat, orchestrated by the omnipresent CAE.

But what of the rebels, the outliers, the ones who dare to color outside the lines? Those artists who have a vision that doesn't align with the 'approved' aesthetic or sentiment? The CAE, with its vast network of informers (often referred to as the "Artful Watchers"), ensures that such deviations don't go unnoticed. The moment an artist veers from the path, they are summoned. First-time offenders are guided to the re-education camps, where they undergo an intensive year of 'creative alignment.' Here, the artists are exposed to the "true essence" of Unicornian art and are encouraged to embrace its harmonious nature.

But woe betide those who relapse into their 'dissident' ways. For them, the journey is more terminal. A second violation results in the artist's transition into oblivion - a shadowy realm where creativity is said to be not just curated but completely stifled.

The CAE's grip on Unicornian art might appear stringent, but its proponents argue it's for the greater good. After all, in a world where kindness, empathy, and mother nature are the bedrocks of society, shouldn't art reflect those very ideals? So, with every brushstroke and every note played, Unicornia endeavors to craft not just art, but a mirror to its own fantastical dreamscape.

The thought of such homogeneity might send chills down the spines of those stuck in the past, ensnared in the obsolete concepts of individual freedom and human rights. They may fret about the death of creativity or the possible stagnation of society. But in the world of Unicornia, such concerns are as irrelevant as an eight-track tape. Here, everyone resonates with the understanding that freedom of speech has become as unnecessary as the dodo, for what need is there to disagree when harmony is our song?

Unicornia: The Matriarchal Utopia - Beyond the Reach of the Patriarchal Echoes

In the land of Unicornia, the morning sun rises to cast its warm gaze upon a realm where females stand unchallenged. Yet, even amidst this matriarchal landscape, the phantom tendrils of patriarchal influence threaten to ensnare the heart of this utopia.

Although men have been relegated to the shadows of public life, vestiges of their influence remain. It's seen in the invisible glass ceilings, the subtle dismissals of female prowess, and the remnants of antiquated gender expectations. These are echoes of a time when payphones were common, a stark contrast to the smartphone-driven society of today.

At the helm of Unicornia's governance stands the indomitable Council of Leaders, an all-female consortium responsible for guiding daily life and even orchestrating matches among citizens. In Unicornia, the once treasured concept of romantic love has been rendered obsolete, replaced by the Council's calculated pairings, which, while efficient, have become tools of control. Love's absence, once a symbol of emancipation, now represents a new form of bondage.

Counteracting these lingering patriarchal influences is the formidable "Patriarchy Patrol." Tasked with a mission to root out all vestiges of masculine influence, they are the shield against a past that Unicornia strives to outgrow. Boys displaying masculine traits undergo a regimen of female hormones, encapsulating their creed: "Equity at all costs."

Unicornia's vision of masculinity has undergone a transformation. Under the combined guidance of the Council of Leaders and the Patriarchy Patrol, the ideal man in this society reflects the Gamma male characteristics, albeit with notable modifications.

The Gamma male in Vox Day's socio-sexual hierarchy typically stands outside the dominance paradigm, often daydreaming of acceptance and respect. Yet, Unicornia's version of the Gamma male has been carefully curated to eliminate any disruptive intellectual curiosity. They've become docile contributors to the societal tapestry, embodying the society's commitment to obliterate traditional gender roles.

Physicality in Unicornia also champions a departure from yesteryears. Muscularity, a symbol of old-world masculinity, has been replaced with a soft, rounded form. Hormonal checks are routine for the Unicornian Gamma, ensuring any inkling of heightened testosterone is promptly neutralized, further reinforcing the state's commitment to a gender-neutral appearance.

Equally revolutionary is Unicornia's approach to the female form. The iconic hourglass figure, once celebrated worldwide, is now taboo. From early childhood, females undergo hormonal treatments to render them nearly indistinguishable from their male counterparts. Makeup, an erstwhile tool for artistic expression, has been banned, and the Patriarchy Patrol enforces this with utmost rigor. Should a female's physique deviate from state standards, such as in breast size, corrective surgeries are mandated.

But the efforts don't stop at the physical. Mental alignment is fostered through equity affirmations, affirming commitment to the Gamma ethos, ensuring that every individual understands and embraces their role in this new order.

However, it's not all strict governance and control. There exists a vibrant, underlying chant, echoing throughout the cities of Unicornia, celebrating feminine power. Each school day begins with students pledging allegiance to this chant, a clarion call for unity and equity.

"Unity in femininity, strength in our identity, Rise above, break the mold, let our story be told. No need for the masculine, in sisterhood we trust, In the power of the feminine, in equity, we thrust."

It's a potent reminder of their history, and the society they continue to build, rooted in matriarchal values and a fervent rejection of the masculine.

Despite the challenges, life in Unicornia persists. With the Council of Leaders and the Patriarchy Patrol steering the ship, the vision remains clear: a society where equity reigns supreme and antiquated norms are left in the annals of history.

THE FORBIDDEN DANCE OF HETERONORMATIVITY IN UNICORNIA'S SYMPHONY OF FLUIDITY

In the paradise that is Unicornia, where binary is not only just a number system but a relic of a bygone era, rigid notions of sex and sexuality have gracefully swirled into oblivion. Here, the very idea of a man and a woman locked in an exclusive relationship is seen with the same incredulity as a fish deciding to live in a tree.

Enter Radiant Rey, the Unicornian embodiment of fluidity, swinging to the harmonious beats of attraction wherever they may lead, unbounded by the suffocating shackles of 'male' and 'female'. Just as the birds don't concern themselves with which direction the wind is blowing, Rey doesn't find themselves tethered to trivialities like gender. It's all fluid, much like their morning drink made from rainbows and ethically sourced unicorn tears.

Ah, but this harmonious fluidity did not come naturally to all. Once upon a time, there were some, gasp, who expressed an exclusive attraction to the opposite sex. Luckily, Unicornia's ever-watchful Patriarchy Patrol swoops down on these defiant hetero-dwellers. Imagine their shock when faced with the inconceivable idea of someone desiring just one gender! It's like preferring only one color of the rainbow. Sacrilege!

Now, these 'rebels' are not ostracized, oh no! Unicornia, with its boundless compassion, ushers them into the "Hetero Healing Hubs". Here, they are gently re-educated about the joys of a free-flowing spectrum of love. Lessons include watching ethereal dance performances where dancers, donning feathered tutus, waltz with shadows to showcase the beauty of gender fluidity.

And should their beliefs prove to be stubbornly rooted, there's always the backup plan: a delightful cocktail of hormones, served in a recycled chalice, to correct any 'imbalances'. After all, why settle for monochrome when you can embrace the spectrum?

Radiant Rey's evenings often resound with conversations, over mugs of insect-cocoa, about the absurdity of a world where 'boy' and 'girl' were once distinct categories. Friends gather, regaling tales of yesteryears, where the Patriarchy Patrol had to intervene and rescue some poor soul from the perils of heteronormativity.

In the heart of Unicornia, as Rey drifts into a dreamless sleep, enveloped in the soft embrace of their ambiguity-certified bedspread, there's a comforting thought: In a world where the borders of gender have evaporated like morning mist, Unicornia stands as a beacon, ensuring that even attractions are never, ever binary. Here, the only binaries that exist are in dusty old history books, often giggled at during readings under the moonlit skies. Ah, Unicornia, where freedom means being everything and nothing, all at once.

Synchronized Symphonies & Fluid Love: Unicornia's Dance of Mating

Part I: Taming Love's Whimsical Waltz

The chaotic flirtations of the heart? Relegated to the faded pages of antiquity, sequestered in the archives alongside myths of a spherical Earth. The Council, with its limitless insight, has alchemized the messy business of procreation into a precision spectacle via the grand 'Unicornian Conception Carousel'. This majestic apparatus assures that progeny are not accidents of emotional impulse, but masterpieces meticulously sculpted from the digital threads of data and equality, scrutinized beneath the relentless stare of the Council's omniscient algorithms.

Physical pleasure? A forbidden relic of yesteryear. Instead, once the Council mandates a pairing, the selected duo embarks on the surreal 'Algorithmic Amalgamation Altar'. In this ceremony devoid of physical contact, they observe the sterile dance where their genetic destinies merge. Physical romance? An outlawed notion, aggressively monitored and quashed by the vigilant Patriarchy Patrol.

PART II: SCULPTING THE FLUID TAPESTRY OF UNICORNIA

In Unicornia, population management is an exquisite ballet, meticulously choreographed by the Council of Equitable Bio-genesis. Here, fluid identities replace outdated heteronormativity.

The Reproductive Lottery transcends mere chance, evolving into a gala where citizens anxiously anticipate the Council's pronouncements on their next partners, potentially pairing with Neutro Nick or Radiant Rey.

Fashion in Unicornia revisits the egalitarian spirit of the Cultural Revolution. Every citizen dons the same outfit—a charming, earth-toned tunic crafted from recycled plant fibers, adorned with a unicorn embracing Mother Earth. Hats, reminiscent of the classic Mao cap, bear eco-conscious slogans like "Hug a Tree, Not Egos," and "Mother Earth Over Mere Mortals," promoting a unified societal fabric.

This uniformity in attire is not just fashion; it's a declaration, a collective homage to the Council's ecological ethos. In Unicornia, personal style is extinct, replaced by a communal aesthetic that champions unity and green fidelity.

Even hair, once a vibrant tapestry of self-expression, adheres to strict regulations. Inspired by the 1920's flappers, every head flaunts a sleek, bobbed cut, uniformly dyed in a nondescript shade of grey, approved by the Council to ensure no individual outshines another. Any deviant hair hue swiftly meets the corrective gaze of the Patriarchy Patrol, with offenders re-educated at the Bureau of Aesthetic Conformity and Chromatic Compliance through hormone treatments ensuring conformity.

Part III: The Harmony of Algorithmic Love and Population Artistry

The Council's decrees are not mere isolated edicts but intricately woven into the fabric of Unicornian society, where algorithmic romance and population control intertwine seamlessly.

Each algorithmic match ensures that the population mirrors the core values of diversity and fluidity, supporting institutions like the Non-Masculinity Museums and Rehabilitation Centers to keep the populace perpetually enlightened.

In Unicornia, the volatile waves of raw emotion have been calmed into a serene flow of orchestrated love. Population management is an art form, each policy, each union, each birth a stanza in the symphony of the Privilege Clock, synchronizing life's rhythm to a march of flawless equality.

Oh, Unicornia, a land where yesteryear's chaotic love is supplanted by the tranquil tempo of compliance! Here, tales of love's fiery zeal and unbridled passion are recounted with amusement—relics of a forgotten era. Now, the population is not merely a number but a poetic expression of satirical finesse and societal artistry. Welcome to a realm where the pursuit of equity has transformed into a splendid parody of itself.

THE ALCHEMY OF UNITY: CRAFTING THE MONOETHNIC MOSAIC OF UNICORNIA

In the vibrant tapestry of Unicornia, the zenith of societal evolution manifests not only in the realms of identity and fashion but also in the profound unity of its people. Embracing the ultimate dream of a homogenized utopia, Unicornia pioneers the dawn of a new race, a splendid fusion of all ethnicities, a singular, harmonious blend that transcends the ancient divides of black, white, brown, and Asian. This monumental achievement in human history is overseen by the esteemed "Committee for Racial Harmony and Genetic Unity" (CRHGU).

The CRHGU, a beacon of progressive thought and genetic artistry, operates with a vision that is as noble as it is audacious: to sculpt a populace devoid of racial divisions, a people unified in their diversity. Through their groundbreaking work, the committee ensures that every newborn Unicornian is a living mosaic, embodying the rich tapestry of human heritage. The race, as known in the bygone era of division and discord, ceases to exist; in its place, a new lineage rises, one that is intrinsically bound to the ethos of Unicornia — unity in diversity, diversity in unity.

Under the watchful guidance of the CRHGU, Unicornia's genetic policies are not mere acts of regulation but are celebrated rituals of unity. The committee meticulously crafts the genetic blueprint of the future, ensuring that each citizen is a testament to the collective heritage of humanity. Their work transcends the mere physical, weaving into the very DNA of the populace the ideals of equality and mutual respect.

The CRHGU's initiatives extend beyond the biological, influencing every facet of Unicornian life. Their annual "Genetic Harmony Festival" is a spectacle of unity, where citizens gather to celebrate their shared heritage and the dissolution of old racial boundaries. Here, amidst the joyous revelries, the committee unveils the "Mosaic of Unity" — a dynamic genetic portrait showcasing the seamless blend of the world's ethnicities within the Unicornian populace.

In the classrooms, the CRHGU's curriculum on "Genetic Unity and Cultural Diversity" shapes young minds, educating them on the historical divides of race and the triumphant journey towards their eradication. Children grow up understanding not the concept of race as a separator but as a historical footnote, a relic of a less enlightened age.

In the luminous dawn of Unicornia's new era, the visage of a Unicornian emerges as a beacon of the utopia's ideals. Crafted under the meticulous guidance of the CRHGU, each citizen boasts a complexion and features reminiscent of Dwayne Johnson — a warm, sun-kissed hue that speaks to a blend of the world's ethnicities. However, it's in the subtleties of their form that the true Unicornian ethos shines through.

Remember though, gone are the overt displays of muscles and traditional markers of masculinity, just as the pronounced curves and distinctions of femininity have faded into the annals of history. In their place, a new physique has been sculpted, one that embodies Unicornia's commitment to eradicating the old binaries.

This nuanced evolution in appearance is a reflection of Unicornia's broader mission: to transcend beyond the superficial divides that once fragmented humanity. The CRHGU, in its infinite wisdom, has engineered a populace where physicality is harmonized with the ethos of unity and diversity. Each citizen, while bearing a resemblance to an admired figure of the old world in complexion and facial harmony, stands as a unique embodiment of Unicornia's revolutionary ideals.

Their bodies, free from the constraints of historical physical ideals, reflect the societal shift towards a more inclusive, egalitarian community. In Unicornia, the beauty of the human form is celebrated not for its adherence to outdated standards, but for its reflection of the collective spirit. The Unicornian appearance, with its gentle nod to the familiar yet a bold leap into the new, is a visual symphony of the world's heritage, seamlessly integrated into a single, unified race.

Thus, Unicornia stands as a testament to what humanity can achieve when it transcends its primitive segregations, guided by the visionary hand of the Committee for Racial Harmony and Genetic Unity. In this realm, equity has found its truest expression, not merely as an aspiration but as a living, breathing reality.

The Macabre Museum of the Antiquated: An Eerie Reminder

Within the pulsing heart of Unicornia, where the ethereal scent of matriarchy mingles with a tangible eeriness, stands The Museum of the Antiquated. Not merely an institution, but rather a dark mirror reflecting a grotesque past over-shadowed by patriarchy.

As visitors meander through the dimly lit corridors, their steps echoing ominously, they're drawn inexorably to the "Hall of Shapes." Here, vast cages loom, each one bathed in a ghastly light. Within, bred under the Council's watchful and unrelenting gaze, stand the "artifacts" of a bygone era: V-shaped men and hourglass females, products of selective breeding, their sole purpose to serve as living reminders of a distorted past.

"The Hourglass Women," reads a plaque, its words dripping with disdain, "Once subject to torturous devices, these females were thought to be the peak of femininity." Nearby, a V-man, every sinewy muscle on grotesque display, stands next to his description: "The V-Men – Hours in primitive 'gyms,' all to achieve an illusion of strength and virility."

Whispers of horror ripple through the audience. "Why did they do this to themselves?" Visitors' eyes, glinting with a mix of pity and horror, rest on a sculpture of a woman, forever trapped in towering heels, "The sacrifices of vanity."

"In a decision stamped with unanimous absurdity, the all-wise Councils agreed to artificially produce living specimens—perfect replicas of archaic human forms, every few years, just for the exhibit. Titled 'Feed the Relics!', this display features a riotous twist. Attendees, brimming with perverse delight, are handed skewers of lab-grown meat to feed these live, breathing relics. As they toss morsels into eagerly waiting mouths, the spectacle turns the grotesque dial up a notch. The attendees marvel at the 'vintage' hourglass and V-shaped physiques, and remain happy about their over hormonally infused, gamma-derived soft bodies, grateful they've evolved past such bizarre biological blueprints.

The chilling "Hall of the Oppressed" is next, a cavalcade of advertisements, films, and dusty magazines, painting a world ensnared in rigid gender norms. Onlookers shake their heads, a collective disbelief echoing, "Could society truly have been so backward?"

Amidst the shadows of retrospection and the echoing silence of the opulent oppression, there winks a sliver of humor in the enclave known as "The Role Reversal." It's here that the visitors, encumbered hearts pulsating with the rhythm of bygone atrocities, allow themselves a brief escape into the realm of ludicrous antiquity.

The air, still tinged with the solemn murmurs of history, vibrates with a new frequency as visitors find themselves ensconced in archaic patriarchal rituals. Their faces, canvases of incredulous amusement, are transformed as they adorn themselves in the layers of makeup once considered the arsenal of the 'fairer sex.' Crimson lips and darkened eyes draw forth chuckles and reflections— "Was beauty truly this paint-laden masquerade?" they ponder, each stroke of the brush a brush with a painted past.

The echoes of laughter meld with the clinking of weights, the iron taste of the ancient pursuit of virility lingering in the air. Visitors grasp the cold metal, their limbs mimicking the archaic dance of muscle and might. "Did this metallic dance truly encapsulate manhood?" resonates amongst the rustling whispers, each lift a fleeting embrace with the primitive valor of yesteryears.

The scent of leather and engine oil infiltrates the air as visitors sink into the plush seats of sports and luxury cars, the once-coveted chariots of masculine prowess. The rumble of engines is met with a symphony of satirical mirth. "Was speed and extravagance the ultimate aphrodisiac?" their laughter inquires, each rev a satirical salute to the vehicular vanities of the past.

Each humorous interaction is a light-hearted waltz with the shadows of a gendered history, a momentary escape into the maze of laughable legacies. The theatrical embrace of the patriarchal pantomime serves as both a comical interlude and a reflective mirror, causing ripples of laughter laced with the underlying musings on the follies of foregone eras.

The absurdity of these once-cherished rituals brings forth not just laughter but also contemplative smiles, a kaleidoscope of reflections on the transformative journey of societal norms. As the veil of humor gradually recedes, leaving behind the echoing chuckles intertwined with the vestiges of patriarchal paradigms, the visitors carry forward a renewed perspective, the satirical interplay a beacon illuminating the evolving dance between the yin and yang of human existence.

The amusement, though ephemeral, leaves a lasting imprint, an amalgamation of humor and enlightenment, allowing the visitors to savor the remnants of comedic reprieve as they continue their journey through the shadows and lights of Unicornia.

Exiting the museum, visitors are met with a juxtaposition: a radiant mural of Unicornia's ascension, where empowered women and enlightened men stride side-by-side. A society born from the ashes of its grim past, it serves as a poignant reminder: to value equity, lest the chains of history bind us once more.

SEASONS OF SOLITUDE: THE LOCKDOWN LITURGY OF UNICORNIA

Ah, and what story of Unicornia would be complete without mention of their famed Lockdown Festivals, those grand affairs of communal solitude, a social paradox birthed from the ashes of the great pandemic of 2020 to 2023? You see, in Unicornia, the mercurial moods of Mother Nature dictate the rhythm of life, not just the blooming of flowers or the migration of birds, but even the societal routines of its soft, round citizens.

Whenever the sun decides to throw a tantrum, turning up its heat a notch too high, or when the winter winds decide to howl with an unnerving intensity, Unicornia enacts its seasonal lockdowns. A retreat from the extremities of nature, a hibernation of sorts. These aren't the dreary, life-sapping lockdowns of the old world; they are considered festivals, a season of inward celebration, where every citizen is a willing participant in this grand act of environmental conservation.

The lockdown is a siren song, beckoning Unicornians to their eco-pods, each citizen cocooning in their personal spaces like an overfed caterpillar ready to metamorphose into a butterfly. They do not resist; they embrace it with the joy of a child embarking on a long-awaited vacation. After all, freedom of thought is a burden long shed, a relic of a less enlightened time, a time before the Great Wokeness.

Each night, under the pastel-hued Unicornian sky, the citizens participate in the Lockdown Liturgy. They stand by their pod windows, palms pressed against the cool, recycled glass, and chant in unison the praises of the lockdown. It's a haunting melody that sweeps across the cities, a lullaby whispered to the sleeping animals in the former suburbs.

Of course, respect for the lockdown is non-negotiable. It's a commitment, a solemn oath each citizen swears to the Council of Leaders. Stepping outside without the necessary clearance and papers is viewed as a blasphemous act, a sacrilege against the very fabric of Unicornian society. The punishment is fittingly severe — a year-long period of reflection within the confines of the Society Correction Facilities on the first offense. A repeat offense is rewarded with a one-way ticket to oblivion, a tragic end no citizen dares to envision.

In Unicornia, to question the Council is unthinkable, to disobey their rules, unforgivable. And so, under the benevolent despotism of the Council, life in Unicornia dances to the tune of the seasonal lockdowns. A dance that unfolds in the solitude of their pods, a tribute to Mother Nature, an offering to the wisdom of their Leaders, an anthem of compliance and conformity echoing across the soft, round contours of their brave, new world.

GASTRONOMY IN UNICORNIA: A FEAST OF HUMILITY AND INSECTS IN UNICORNIA

The culinary landscape has undergone a transformation as profound as its societal norms. The succulent steaks, the smoky barbecues, the dairy-rich delights — they all exist now as tales of a barbaric past, relics of a time when humanity's carnivorous inclinations held sway. In their place, a new diet has taken root, one that echoes the enlightened ethos of this brave new world.

In the utopian cradle of Unicornia, the gastronomic canvas is a radiant display of ecological sanctity and nutritional enlightenment. A ban has been gloriously bestowed upon the concoctions of hedonistic libations, yes, even the most innocent of non-alcoholic spirits, leaving the inhabitants swimming in a sea of purifying elixirs. The once-beloved brews, wines and spirits of the past now dwell in the annals of forbidden indulgences, their absence a celestial nod to the immaculate sobriety of Unicornian existence. Even the whisper of a non-alcoholic beer elicits a symphony of Unicornian gasps, the very idea a sacrilegious dance with the shadows of intemperate antiquity.

In this harmonious symphony of sustainability, the culinary palette is a futuristic ballet of lab-concocted nourishment, each bite a hymn sung in praise of resource-efficiency. The meals, artistic renditions of eco-friendliness, resonate with the vibrant echoes of the sacred insects, the crowned jewels of Unicornian sustenance.

Oh yes, insects! The creepy-crawlies have ascended from the shadows of nocturnal dread to bask in the gastronomical spotlight, their crunchy exoskeletons the stars of a dining experience steeped in environmental reverence. Beetles, crickets, grasshoppers, each a knight in shining armor on the green battlefield of nutrition, their flavors a divine dance on the enlightened palates of Unicornians.

And it's not just about the protein-rich waltz of these diminutive heroes; it's a sonnet of minimal ecological footprints, a celestial caress to Mother Nature herself. The consuming of these chirping crusaders is a satirical toast to the harmonious interplay between humanity and nature, their crispy bodies a crunchy ode to the ecological utopia that is Unicornia.

The culinary odyssey of Unicornia is a kaleidoscope of flavors and ethics, a continuous waltz between innovative nourishment and planetary love. Each meal is an experience, a tableau vivant of progressive ideals and eco-consciousness, each crunch a whisper of thanks to the environmental saviors gracing the Unicornian plates.

Public meals are a solemn affair, a moment to contemplate the sins of past generations and to give thanks for the enlightened diet of the present. Before partaking in their insectuous feast, each citizen must utter the Mealtime Mantra, an affirmation of love for Mother Earth and commitment to the great cause of equity. The mantra goes as follows:

"We eat for the Earth, we dine for Justice, our plates a testament to Sustainability."

"Cows are for the cruel, Beetles are our boon, in Unity with Nature, we will thrive."

"Insects over Indulgence, Equity over Excess, we break bread with the bugs, for a World reborn."

"Beef is the banner of White Supremacy; we reject it with fervor, embracing the feast of Fairness and Foliage."

As the mantra echoes around the dining halls, a shiver of collective guilt and gratitude washes over the citizens. They remember the wastefulness and cruelty of the past, the barbaric consumption of meat and animal products, and they shudder. Then they look down at their meals, at the crunchy beetles or the rich, protein-packed algae loaf, and they feel a surge of pride, a confirmation of their commitment to this enlightened path.

Overseeing these public dining rituals are of course, the members of our Patriarchy Patrol, their vigilant eyes scanning for any deviation from the norm. Any citizen who fails to recite the Mealtime Mantra, who dares to consume their food without acknowledging the sacrifices of the past and the wisdom of the present, faces a hefty fine. The rules of Unicornian gastronomy are as stringent as their dietary restrictions.

And so, every meal in Unicornia becomes a testament to their progress, a reaffirmation of their societal ideals. It's a gastronomical dance choreographed to the tune of their new dietary ethos, a merry jingle of crunching beetles and grateful hearts, a symphony of sustainable eating that feeds not just the body, but also the soul of Unicornia.

The Chronicles of Mediocrity: The Un-Meritocratic Utopia - A Satirical Symphony of Sameness

Once upon a time, in the days of old, meritocracy roared in the hearts of men and women. It sparked innovation, fueled competition, and embraced achievement. But in Unicornia, such ancient, distasteful concepts have been tucked neatly under the bed of history, right beside Ayn Rand's individualistic masterpieces. In the pastel-colored, round-edged world of Unicornia, mediocrity is the intoxicating elixir that feeds the soul of society.

Under the wise and watchful eye of the Great Council of Fairness, a beacon of harmonious humdrum, Unicornia revels in the sweet symphony of sameness. "All are equal; none shall rise above," echoes across the flat plains, carried by the wind, sung by the birds, inscribed in the heart of every Unicornian. The pursuit of excellence is seen as an unsightly blemish, an outrageous rebellion against the comforting embrace of ordinariness.

The world of work, once a tumultuous sea of ambition and innovation, is now a placid pond reflecting the dull gray skies of uniformity. The brilliant engineer, who once dreamt of soaring skyscrapers and groundbreaking machinery, now oils the cogs of mediocrity. Her inventive spirit, tamed by the collective will, contentedly hums the hymn of sameness. The inspired author, whose pen once birthed worlds and defied the gods, now churns out volumes of perfectly ordinary prose. The exhilarating highs and devastating lows of his narratives have been leveled out to create a literary landscape as flat and unremarkable as a Unicornian plain.

The spirit of Ayn Rand's hero, Equality 7-2521, who dared to kindle the light of knowledge in the gloom of ignorance, has no place in Unicornia. His bold pursuits of innovation, his thirst for individual glory, these are considered dangerous sparks that could set ablaze the peaceful fields of sameness. In Unicornia, the heady heights of personal achievement have been gently lowered to the comfortable level of the crowd. Every day is a celebration of the ordinary, a toast to the comfortably average, a merry jig in the lush, level fields of mediocrity. Welcome to Unicornia, the un-meritocratic utopia, where no one dares to be different, and everyone delights in being wonderfully, delightfully, emphatically the same.

MOTHER NATURE'S CLASSROOM: THE HARMONIOUS HOMOGENY OF EDUCATION IN UNICORNIA

Oh, the boundless wisdom of Unicornia! Before the innocent souls embark on their enlightening journey through education at the tender age of five, they are graced with the profound enlightenment of the esteemed Council of Fairness. Yes, for one whole year, their little minds are showered with the sacred truths of equality, a sanctified ritual to ensure the remnants of the old patriarchal notion of 'equality of opportunity' are dutifully eradicated.

Every day, in these revered gatherings, children are bathed in the glorious light of absolute equality. Their young minds are sculpted by the artisan hands of the Council, carving into their consciousness the dangers lurking in the shadows of competitive spirit. "Competition is the ghost of the antiquated," the Council would lovingly whisper, "Winning is the song of the misguided".

The notion of 'winning' is presented as a treacherous path, a forbidden dance with the demonic whispers of individual achievement. "In Unicornia, we don't rise by standing on the shoulders of others," they are taught, "We rise by blending into the harmonious choir of collective sameness".

Such teachings are the nourishing nectar to the blooming flowers of tomorrow. The Council, with their ever-watchful eyes and nurturing hands, ensure that every seedling grows not towards the sun, but rather entwined with one another, creating a seamless tapestry of unified existence, free from the perilous cliffs of ambition and the treacherous waters of distinction.

In the pastel-colored halls of Unicornian schools, the words "independent thought" and "debate" are now dusty relics tucked away in the attic of forgotten lexicons. These ancient concepts have no place in the corridors that echo with harmonious hymns of unanimity. There's a singular, unequivocal truth that resonates in the air - Mother Nature is paramount. In the world of Unicornia, this is not a fact to be questioned but a divine edict to be revered.

In the glorious realm of Unicornia, education is not a mere institution; it's an artful pageant, a harmonious waltz of homogenized intellects. A mesmerizing choreography where minds pirouette in perfect alignment to the universal rhythm of uniformity. Here, students glide through their academic journey not with the clunky steps of critical thinking but with the seamless flow of synchronized sentiment.

However, on rare occasions, a daring dancer might misstep, introducing a jarring note of rogue reasoning into this grand performance. The atmosphere tenses. Eyebrows arch. The hallowed halls of knowledge resonate with an incredulous silence. And then, like clockwork, the loyal guardians of groupthink spring into action. The audacious thinker is encircled, ensnared within a ring of righteous peers.

They begin their chant, voices escalating from a whisper to a crescendo, a melodic safeguard against the insidious threat of independent thought: "Mother nature is paramount! In her embrace, we thrive. By her law, we abide. Mother Nature, eternal and wise!" Each word is a strand, weaving a protective net to catch and recalibrate any straying sentiment. Top of Form

The dissenter is then promptly whisked away to the benevolent bosom of the authorities. After all, in Unicornia, divergence is seen not as defiance but as a deviation to be gently corrected. The misguided student is sent for several months of re-education, a therapeutic process designed to realign their thoughts with the harmonious hum of the Unicornian worldview.

In these sacred havens of homogenized learning, the very notion of intellectual stimulation, the old-world thrill of discovering a new theorem, the joy of unraveling the mysteries of the universe, are considered needless luxuries. Instead, minds are molded to the comforting shape of the average, the safe cocoon of the unexceptional. And so, the lanterns of intellect are dimmed to a soft, pleasing glow, harmonizing perfectly with the gentle light of Unicornian mediocrity. This is education in Unicornia, a world where individual brilliance gives way to the shared, soothing melody of shared thinking, where the only guiding star is the gentle, nurturing spirit of Mother Nature herself.

The Level Playing Fields of Sports in Unicornia

In the softly lit vistas of Unicornia, sports arenas exist, not as theatres of human strength and competition, but as venues for the celebration of moderation and equity. You see, in this utopian world, the joy of sports is untethered from the concepts of winning, losing, or individual prowess. It's an ethos so deeply ingrained that it begins from the moment a Unicornian infant is assigned their sex. Too much masculinity is considered a threat to the soft, round fabric of Unicornia. This ensures that from their very first breath, Unicornians are set on a path that upholds the cherished values of their society.

In the utopian realm of Unicornia, sporting excellence takes on a different hue. Here, the landscape of sports champions the truly egalitarian.

Before setting foot on the sacred fields of play, every aspirant, regardless of age, must first clear the Performance Potential Assessment. Contrary to what one might expect, this isn't a test of one's athletic prowess. Instead, it seeks to gauge mediocrity. The golden standard? A score nestled between the 9th and 24th percentiles. Only these chosen individuals are anointed as worthy participants.

However, the pursuit of fairness does not end there. Unicornia, in its boundless wisdom, recognizes the perils of average. Thus, individuals audacious enough to even graze the average range, beginning at the 25th percentile are expressly forbidden from participating. After all, the audacity of some to be merely average! The realm believes in the brilliance of mediocrity, making it the shining beacon on the field of play. For those teetering on the brink of the average, irrespective of their gender or anatomy, a simple message resounds: Unicornia's fields are no place for such lofty overachievers.

But what of the exceptional? The outstanding few that threaten to plunge the domain into the abyss of toxic competition? Fear not, for Unicornia has it covered. These athletic anomalies don't just face score-based exclusions. Oh no, the process is far more sophisticated. They undergo extensive hormone evaluations and face the esteemed Council of Athletic Equity. This council, a revered assembly of scholars from the illustrious disciplines of Non-Competitive Sports Science and Inclusive Game Theory, holds a singular purpose. Their sacred duty? To shield the pristine world of sports from the taint of ambition or inherent skill, ensuring that the altar of uniform mediocrity remains unsullied.

Athletic events in Unicornia thus become a celebration of the mediocre, a symposium of sameness where everyone competes at the same level of sub-mediocrity. The games are not about winning or losing; they are about collective participation and mutual validation. In the end, everyone receives a trophy made of recycled, body-positive clay, symbolizing the harmonious union of mediocrity and fairness.

This approach to sports represents the very ethos of Unicornian society, where equity isn't just an ideal; it's a lived reality, enshrined in every law, embraced in every heart, and celebrated with every mediocre swing of a bat.

In the diverse world of Unicornian sports, there's no room for individual sports. No sprinters racing against the wind, no tennis players battling it out in the summer sun. These sports, with their spotlight on individual achievement, are considered dangerous relics of a less enlightened age. Instead, team sports dominate the arenas, their inherent camaraderie and cooperation a perfect fit for Unicornia's ethos.

But the real magic of Unicornian sports lies in the games themselves. There are no winners or losers; each game is a symphony that ends on the harmonious note of a tie. The rules are charmingly unique. If a team leads by two points, players are exchanged to level the field once more. The games ebb and flow in this manner, a dance of perpetual balance, until the score is tied.

This merry carousel of mediocrity, this celebration of average performance, paints a vivid picture of Unicornia's sports landscape. It's a tableau of joyful participation, devoid of competitiveness, of toxic masculinity, of winners and losers. Sports in Unicornia are a testament to their societal values, a world where the thrill of the game isn't marred by the pursuit of victory but enriched by the shared joy of playing in the beautifully average orchestra of athletic mediocrity.

Unicornia's Polite Paradox: Where Satire Meets Silence

In Unicornia, where every word is a hug and every sentence a respectful nod, humor has become a thing of the past. Satirical works, comedies, and anything that might offend the state are promptly banned, placed in the Unicornia Archives of Unpleasantness.

Remember the Patriarchy Patrol? Of course you do! They're back with glittery badges and an unshakable resolve. Patrolling the streets with renewed fervor, they're on a mission to eradicate anything that might cause a giggle or a smirk. They've even developed a special sensor that detects the faintest hint of irony, with an accuracy rate of "pretty good, probably.

The Unicornia University of Utter Niceness (UUUN) has seen a surge of new students, courtesy of the ever-vigilant Patriarchy Patrol. Re-education has never been so polite. Courses have been expanded to include "The Subtleties of Snark Suppression" and "Pun Prevention: A Crash Course."

The Language Code of Unicornia, now mandatory reading material for all, remains a masterpiece of monotony. Displayed on every screen and recited daily by every citizen, it's the bedtime story no child asks for but gets anyway.

Even pets are trained to bark, meow, and tweet with utmost respect.

Humorless holidays and festivals are the highlight of Unicornia's cultural calendar. The annual Unity Unicorns parade is a joyful event, as long as your joy is carefully measured and follows the government-approved Joyfulness Guidelines. Any deviation is handled by the Patriarchy Patrol, who will kindly escort you to the UUUN for an extended vacation.

Leaders and citizens alike continue to live in a state of blissful boredom. They compose epic poems about kindness and sing soulless songs about harmony. But fear not, dear outsider, for Unicornia has its entertainment too: the live broadcasts of the Patriarchy Patrol's daily briefings are the hottest tickets in town. Who knew respect could be so... repetitive?

So, if your taste in literature, art, and comedy has been deemed too lively for Unicornia, take heart! You're in excellent company, with the classics of satire and the entirety of this very work. As the citizens of Unicornia say (in a manner most earnest), "May your words be dull, and your thoughts be orderly!"

Embracing Mother Nature's Harmonic Wisdom: The Grand Redesign of Learning in Unicornia

In the soft-hued expanse of Unicornia, where every heartbeat synchronizes to the rhythm of societal harmony, the unruly sphere of knowledge has undergone a profound metamorphosis. Science, once a hotbed of dispute and uncertainty, dominated by stubborn white males, has been delicately rebranded in the name of Unity and Progress. Out with the old, fraught with disagreement and chaos, and in with the new, brimming with the harmonic wisdom of Mother Nature's Plan.

No more are the days of squabbling scholars and disputatious debates that echoed in the hallowed halls of academia. The ancient, tumultuous quest for truth has been replaced by the serene tranquility of Mother Nature's wisdom, passed down by the all-seeing Council.

The Council, in its all-encompassing wisdom, has unified all fields of knowledge under the comforting umbrella of what we now fondly refer to as "The Universal Knowledge Symphony". This term replaces the old term, science, which we now understand was simply another tool of patriarchal oppression. With this, the Council ensures that the discords of disagreement are forever silenced. All white male scholars, such as the once revered Popper, have been elegantly erased from Unicornian memory, replaced with a harmonious chorus of Universal Knowledge.

In Unicornia, the chaotic cacophony of diverse ideas has been replaced by the sweet melody of unified learning. The mind, once the battlefield of clashing thoughts, has been reprogrammed to sing praises of the Council's Universal Knowledge Symphony. The echo of each shared thought in Unicornia is as predictable as the soothing sound of the council's voice.

Dare to challenge this harmonious symphony? Don't be foolish! Any discordance is met with immediate imprisonment. As we've all been taught, attempting to refute the wisdom of the Council is as pointless as attempting to outshine the sun. This is no place for chaos and uncertainty. Knowledge is no longer a treacherous journey through a jungle of conflicting ideas, but a serene stroll through a well-tended garden, guided by the nurturing hand of the Council.

In Unicornia, the old-fashioned, white male-dominated 'Science' is but a distant memory. All citizens, under the vigilant gaze of the Council, are trained to understand that this is the natural order of things. There's no room for doubt, no room for arguments, and certainly no room for uncertainty. The discourse of old, laden with contesting theories and the harrowing possibility of being wrong, has been replaced by the soothing harmony of unanimous agreement.

In Unicornia, the pursuit of knowledge, once a wild stallion racing headlong into the winds of uncertainty, has been domesticated, harnessed, and set to plow the fields of societal harmony. The rhythm of thought has been orchestrated to align with the Council's grand symphony of Universal Knowledge. Welcome to the land of unified learning, where every thought is a note in the grand composition of the Council, where intellectual chaos is but a fairy-tale from a long-forgotten past.

THE "NOT-A-RELIGION" RELIGION OF UNICORNIA: EMBRACING THE UNQUESTIONABLE FAITH OF MOTHER NATURE

In the all-embracing embrace of Unicornia, where the mere thought of challenging the status quo is as mythical as a two-horned unicorn, the concept of faith has undergone a rebranding as groundbreaking as a pixie learning quantum mechanics. Religion, that antiquated construct once used to explain the unknown and bond communities, has been diplomatically outlawed. Yet, in its wake, the glorious worship of Mother Nature has ascended, not as a religion, but as an undeniable truth.

Dwell not on the irony, dear reader, for in the heart of Unicornia, irony is a luxury no one can afford. The doctrines of yesteryears, rife with deities, myths, and moral compasses, have been gently escorted out, only for the doctrines of "Mother Nature's Benevolence" to take center stage. Yet, this is not a religion. Oh, heavens no! It is merely a way of life, one that just happens to demand utter devotion, unwavering belief, and oh, the occasional ritual (but strictly for environmental reasons, of course).

Mother Nature, unlike the deities of old, doesn't require temples. Instead, her shrines are the very streets of Unicornia, where devout followers can be seen expressing their reverence by hugging trees, whispering apologies to the flowers they inadvertently step on, and occasionally performing the Dance of the Rain Clouds, hoping to prevent the slight drizzle forecasted for Thursday afternoon.

The "Not-a-Religion" religion of Mother Nature is guided, of course, as you know, by the omniscient Council. They, in their infinite wisdom, have deciphered Mother Nature's wishes by reading the subtle signs she provides - like the way the leaves rustle or the precise angle a rainbow arcs. This has nothing to do with old-world divine revelations, mind you. It's purely scientific, as everything in Unicornia tends to be.

Questioning this faith is not just frowned upon, it's downright laughable! Why would anyone challenge the wisdom of a breeze or the judgment of a hummingbird? To even entertain such doubts is to reveal oneself as a non-believer in Mother Nature's grand plan. And while religion is banned, being a non-believer in the "Not-a-Religion" is a crime of the highest order.

A Wake-Up Call from Unicornia to Reality

Leaving behind the satirical shores of Unicornia, we are confronted with a stark realization: Contemporary culture, once a realm of freedom and individuality, is undergoing a profound transformation. This shift is marked by an increasing wave of misguided DEI initiatives that undermine the very principles they aim to uphold.

Previously, in Unicornia, I used extreme satire to highlight the alarming changes in our educational and social paradigms. The narrative depicted a scenario where conventional wisdom and the valued skill of critical thinking are being sidelined. Under the guise of inclusivity, a new orthodoxy has taken hold—one that often stifles debate and real understanding.

This next section of the book discusses why the current approach to DEI must be critically reassessed and the specific challenges that men face in this evolving cultural landscape. It is a call to action, urging us to return to a path that truly honors real diversity of thought and sincere equality.

WHY DEI NEEDS TO DIE FOR A HEALTHY SOCIETY

Imagine a world where the color of your skin or the culture you come from doesn't just define your opportunities but limits them. This is the reality we're facing under the current regime of Diversity, Equity, and Inclusion (DEI), where instead of a melting pot, we're being sorted into separate pots, each simmering in its own stew of identity politics. This isn't just about DEI needing to die; it's about recognizing that in trying to fix one form of discrimination, we've birthed another, more insidious one.

THE PARADOX OF DEI

DEI, in its noble quest for inclusivity, has paradoxically become a tool for exclusion, particularly against White and Asian individuals. Under the banner of equity, we see policies that favor one group over another, not based on merit, but as a reparation for historical injustices. But here's the rub: this approach doesn't heal; it divides. It's as if we've forgotten that equality, true equality, means treating everyone with the same measure of respect and opportunity, not doling out privileges based on skin color or ancestry. Equity, as it's currently practiced, is not about leveling the playing field; it's about shifting the goalposts.

The Harm of Equity

This shift towards equity is not just detrimental; it's a societal poison. By focusing on equity over equality, we're telling entire groups of people that they are inherently less capable or more capable based on their race or ethnicity. This isn't just patronizing; it's a direct assault on the principle of individual merit. When we advance someone not because of their skills or achievements but because of their ethnicity, we diminish not just them but the very fabric of our society. We're breeding resentment, not unity.

The Need for a Return to Equality

What we need is a return to equality, where every individual, regardless of their background, can stand on their achievements. This isn't about ignoring history or denying that certain groups have faced, and continue to face, systemic barriers. It's about acknowledging these issues while also recognizing that the solution isn't to reverse the discrimination but to eliminate it altogether. We must focus on uplifting everyone, especially those at the margins of society, not through handouts based on identity but through opportunities that recognize potential wherever it exists.

A Call for MIE

In the wake of DEI's missteps, I propose Meritocracy, Innovation, and Equality (MIE). This isn't just a new acronym; it's a lifeline for a society adrift. MIE champions individual merit, not group identity. It encourages innovation by providing an environment where every idea, from every corner, can flourish. And it holds steadfast to equality, ensuring that every human, regardless of their race, gender, or socio-economic background, has the chance to soar based on their abilities, not their identity.

Meritocracy Now, let's talk meritocracy—where your skills and efforts determine your success, not who you know or the color of your shoelaces. In a true meritocracy, opportunities are like coffee—available to everyone who's up for the grind. It's about rewarding those who put in the effort and excel, ensuring that hard work and talent are the true currency of advancement. This shifts the narrative from a patronizing pat-on-the-back for merely showing up, to a robust handshake for genuinely stepping up. It champions competence and dedication, ensuring that the most capable are those steering the ship—because let's face it, you wouldn't want your neurosurgeon to be picked based on anything but their ability to, quite literally, keep a steady hand under pressure.

Innovation And then there's innovation—the secret sauce that keeps societies thriving. It's about more than just inventing the next big gadget; it's about fostering an environment where new ideas can germinate, and old problems can see new solutions. In a world that celebrates innovation, creativity is the currency and everyone is encouraged to invest. This ensures that progress isn't just a buzzword in annual reports but a tangible reality improving lives across the board. An innovative mindset invites a future where we fix more than we break and where challenges are springboards, not stop signs. After all, if necessity is the mother of invention, let's just say innovation is the cool uncle who shows up with a jetpack.

Equality Remember the term, equality? That notion that all individuals, regardless of sex, gender, and race, deserve an equal chance to rise? It seems we've lost that memo with the current focus on group identity. We need a focus on upliftment that transcends race and gender to include all marginalized groups, including the homeless. The emphasis on class issues, for example, could provide a more unifying and effective framework for addressing social inequalities. This approach recognizes that socio-economic disparities often cut across various demographic lines and addressing these can have a universally beneficial impact. It's about broadening the scope of our efforts to create a society where the primary goal is to elevate everyone, particularly those in the most challenging circumstances, irrespective of their identity markers. This approach fosters a sense of shared human experience and common goals, rather than dividing people into ever-smaller groups based on identity. We're aiming for a balance that respects the unique experiences of all individuals, without losing sight of our collective humanity. This balance is crucial for the sustainable progress and harmony of any society.

Conclusion: From DEI to MIE

The shift from DEI to MIE isn't just necessary; it's urgent. It's about moving from a society that divides to one that unites through shared values and opportunities. It's about ensuring that the ladder of success has rungs for all to climb, not just a select few. In advocating for MIE, we're not just asking for a change in policy; we're calling for a renaissance in how we view and value one another. Let DEI die, not because diversity, equity, and inclusion are bad concepts, but because in their current form, they've lost the very essence of what they were meant to achieve. Let MIE fly, for in its wings, we find the true path toward a society that values each individual not for what they are but for what they can achieve.

The Forgotten Half: Charting the Downfall of Men in Modern Society

What of men in Western culture? While the fictional men of Unicornia serve as an exaggerated satire, reflecting certain societal perceptions, the genuine challenges faced by men in the contemporary world are pressing and undeniable. These struggles, deeply entrenched in the complexities of today's society, deserve our collective attention and action.

I think it's crucial that we take a step back and look at the wider landscape. It's important to recognize and understand some challenges that men face in contemporary society. These challenges, often overlooked or misunderstood, significantly shape our paths and can impact how we perceive and achieve success. So, before we dive into strategies for personal growth and accomplishment, let's shed some light here.

Beyond examining the struggles men encounter, it's equally important to highlight the positive contributions men bring to the table. Despite the challenges, many men continue to play crucial roles in various aspects of society, often pushing boundaries and forging paths in areas ranging from scientific advancements to societal reform. These positive contributions are vital and form the core foundation from which many men operate. They shape our communities, impact our world, and help set the stage for future generations. So, as we journey through this book, we'll also take the time to honor and delve into these contributions, acknowledging the strength, resilience, and indomitable spirit of men that can often go unnoticed.

The issues facing men in today's society, I assure you, are no laughing matter. Statistics tell a rather grim tale - according to the American Foundation for Suicide Prevention, men are 3.63 times more likely to commit suicide than women. Men also fall victim to violent crimes at a higher rate, as indicated by the U.S. Bureau of Justice Statistics. When it comes to post-secondary education, men lag behind, with fewer enrollments and graduations compared to their female counterparts. This is a reality we cannot afford to ignore. In the United States, a significant trend has been unfolding in the educational landscape, where women have consistently outperformed men in terms of college graduation rates. This shift began to become noticeable in the mid-1990s, when among individuals aged 25-34, the percentage of women holding a bachelor's degree started to surpass that of their male counterparts.

This trend has only continued to widen. By looking at enrollment figures for the academic year starting in the fall of 2021, data from Statistics Canada highlights a stark disparity: women's enrollment outstripped men's by a notable margin, specifically by 18 percentage points. This gap represents nearly one-fifth of the total student population, illustrating a significant imbalance in higher education gender demographics.

In a world where popular culture often seems hell-bent on painting a picture of men as anything from bumbling idiots to excessively violent beings, it's more important than ever for us to take a balanced and constructive look at masculinity. Ah, popular culture, where men often get to play two primary roles - either we're complete buffoons, unable to tell a diaper from a dustbin, or we're portrayed as senselessly violent, our on-screen demises often accompanied by an excess of blood and gore that could make even a seasoned special effects artist queasy.

In commercials and sitcoms, we often find the familiar trope of the clueless dad. This character is usually seen struggling with simple tasks, much to the amusement of his wife and kids. He burns breakfast, shrinks laundry, and can't for the life of him figure out how to handle a crying baby. I mean, come on! We may not all be perfect at these tasks, but surely we're not all that hapless!

And speaking of curious media phenomena, have you ever noticed how straight white males are apparently so incompetent that they can't land a job in a commercial unless it's to play the bumbling fool? Next time you flick through channels, play a little game called 'Spot the Competent Straight White Male.' Spoiler alert: you'll have better luck finding a unicorn at a narwhal's pool party. It's as if there's a secret casting rule: "Must be able to trip over flat surfaces and exhibit confusion at a toaster." Really, it's a wonder how we ever managed to invent the wheel, let alone run companies or countries.

And then, of course, there's the movie industry. Ah, Hollywood, where a man's life is as expendable as the popcorn you're munching on in the theater. Men are constantly meeting gruesome ends on screen. From gangster movies to war epics, it's as if the screenwriters are holding a competition on who can knock off characters in the most imaginatively violent ways. It's all fun and games until you realize that such portrayals can perpetuate harmful stereotypes, reinforcing a distorted and overly simplistic view of masculinity.

And isn't it peculiar, the glaring lack of equity when it comes to the demise of characters in movies? While men frequently meet their ends in the most gruesome and dramatic ways imaginable, the multitude of women facing similar fates is absent. It's almost as if Hollywood has decided that men are the disposable heroes, destined to be dispatched in increasingly creative spectacles of doom. This selective approach to character termination not only skews perceptions of risk and sacrifice but also subtly suggests that only certain lives are expendable for the sake of entertainment. Isn't it high time that the screenwriters' guild updates its playbook? Maybe they could sprinkle a little more 'equality' into those action-packed finales!

These portrayals can contribute to a warped perception of men, with damaging implications for both individuals and society. In reality, men, like any other group, are diverse, with a wide range of skills, characteristics, and emotions. We are complex beings, not one-dimensional caricatures.

And let's not forget the mandatory subplot in every second movie: the bad father. It's as if Hollywood has an unspoken rulebook where every script must include a man being a terrible spouse or a father figure who's either absent or, worse, villainous. Meanwhile, male antagonists apparently skipped every class except Chauvinism 101, only to be schooled dramatically by a female character in a grand display of physical or intellectual dominance. It's a storyline so reliable you could set your watch to it. It's gotten to the point where if a movie dad isn't neglecting his kids, you might start wondering if you walked into the wrong theater. It's high time we ask: are scriptwriters just out of original ideas, or is there a secret warehouse where these tired tropes are recycled, repackaged, and shipped out for our consumption?

As we embark on this exploration of the challenges and victories that accompany the journey of being a man in the 21st century, it is imperative to begin with a sense of perspective. It's crucial to acknowledge the tremendous contributions men have made to society, many of which have been significant yet often overlooked. Let's take a moment to appreciate the immeasurable positive impact men have had over the years.

PIONEERS OF PROGRESS

Throughout history, men have played a critical role as innovators and pioneers in a wide range of fields. They've made groundbreaking contributions to science, technology, politics, arts, literature, and social reforms. Men like Isaac Newton, Albert Einstein, and Nikola Tesla laid the foundation for modern physics and engineering. Literary giants like William Shakespeare and Mark Twain have influenced generations with their wit and wisdom. Figures like Martin Luther King Jr., Mahatma Gandhi, and Nelson Mandela have been stalwarts of social change, advocating for equality and human rights.

CHAMPIONS OF CHANGE

Men have also been instrumental in driving societal change. They have challenged stereotypes, broken barriers, and championed causes that range from gender equality to environmental conservation. Men like Frederick Douglass, an abolitionist, fought against slavery and for the rights of African Americans. Others like David Attenborough have dedicated their lives to educating the world about the importance of preserving our environment.

ADVOCATES FOR EQUALITY

Men have played a vital role in supporting and promoting women's rights, often standing side by side with women in the fight for gender equality. Men like John Stuart Mill, an influential 19th-century philosopher and political economist, championed women's rights at a time when it was highly controversial. Today, countless men serve as allies, supporting initiatives and policies aimed at promoting gender equality.

PROVIDERS AND PROTECTORS

Men have traditionally been the providers and protectors of their families, a role that carries immense responsibility. They have strived to ensure the safety and well-being of their loved ones, often sacrificing their comfort and desires in the process. The role of men as fathers, mentors, and role models is priceless and continues to be a vital element in the fabric of our society.

Despite these immense contributions, it is true that men's issues often don't receive the same level of attention or support as women's. This isn't to discount the importance of women's causes or the challenges women have historically faced. However, it highlights the need for a more balanced approach to gender-related issues, one that acknowledges the struggles and challenges of both sexes.

Responders in Crisis Men often stand at the forefront during emergencies—whether as firefighters, police officers, or emergency medical technicians. When the power goes out during storms and disasters, it is frequently men who brave the elements to restore order and safety. They work tirelessly in the face of danger to ensure public safety and provide essential services, demonstrating courage and resilience that underpin the stability of communities.

Innovators in Health and Safety Men have been pivotal in advancing public health and safety. From developing life-saving medical technologies and pharmaceuticals to engineering safer buildings and transportation systems, their innovations have saved millions of lives. Men in fields like biotechnology, civil engineering, and epidemiology continue to push the boundaries of what is possible to enhance human health and daily living.

Custodians of Knowledge Men have also been custodians and transmitters of knowledge. As educators, researchers, and scholars, they have been crucial in nurturing the intellectual and cultural growth of societies. Universities, libraries, and research institutions abound with men who dedicate their lives to teaching, discovering, and spreading knowledge, ensuring that each generation is better informed and more curious than the last.

Visionaries in Technology In the realm of technology, men have not only been inventors but also visionaries who have shaped the digital world. Figures like Tim Berners-Lee, who invented the World Wide Web, and entrepreneurs like Steve Jobs, who revolutionized personal computing and mobile communication, have transformed how we live and work. Their visions have spawned entirely new industries, creating jobs and fostering economic growth.

In the evolving world, another set of contemporary issues has risen to prominence for men. A study by the Pew Research Center reveals a growing number of young men displaying a diminished interest in marriage and long-term commitments, a trend some attribute to a shift in societal values and perceptions of masculinity. Additionally, digital distractions, especially video games and online pornography, have become a rising concern. The World Health Organization has even recognized video game addiction as a mental health disorder. This, coupled with the staggering amount of time many young men spend on pornography, often leads to social isolation, desensitization, distorted perceptions of relationships, and an overall decrease in life satisfaction.

Another facet of the contemporary male struggle is the dwindling engagement of men in higher education. As men's enrollments in post-secondary institutions decline, so does their economic mobility and professional opportunities. In turn, this can result in a sense of disillusionment and disengagement from society. Without proper guidance and mentorship, many young men find themselves adrift, lacking purpose or direction.

Masculinity Misjudged: Rebalancing the Narrative"

In recent times, society has increasingly spotlighted the concept of 'toxic masculinity,' often painting broad strokes that unfairly categorize traditional masculine traits as inherently detrimental. This hyperfocus on critiquing masculinity not only distorts the narrative but also overshadows the positive aspects of male contributions. The dialogue has shifted so drastically that it sometimes appears as though many of society's ills are hastily attributed to men, overlooking the complexities of individual behavior and societal dynamics.

The Unbalanced Support System Venturing into any public sphere, whether a local store or engaging with financial services, one often encounters initiatives prominently supporting women's progress, from entrepreneurship to personal well-being. For instance, walking into a local LCBO in Ontario, customers are frequently asked to contribute to women's charities. Similarly, advertisements on banking terminals proudly announce support for female entrepreneurs. While these initiatives are commendable, their visibility starkly contrasts with the comparative lack of similar public support structures for men, inadvertently suggesting that men either already possess sufficient resources or lack equivalent challenges.

The Impact on Men's Perception This skewed portrayal can contribute to a societal narrative that men are invariably part of the problem rather than partners in progress. It perpetuates a sense that any celebration or support of men's issues is either unnecessary or unprogressive. Such a narrative not only stifles honest conversation about the challenges men face but also alienates them from participating in broader societal discussions about gender equality and mutual support.

Need for Support Systems The reality is that men, like any group, face specific challenges that deserve recognition and support—ranging from higher rates of suicide and homelessness to societal pressures of fulfilling the role of the primary provider. Addressing these issues does not diminish the support for women but rather enriches the fabric of societal care by ensuring that all members' needs are acknowledged and addressed. A comprehensive approach where both men's and women's challenges are openly discussed and supported would foster a healthier society where every individual feels valued.

Moving Towards a Balanced Dialogue To move forward, society must cultivate a more balanced dialogue that uplifts all without bias and recognizes the virtues in traditional masculine qualities—such as courage, resilience, and protectiveness—while condemning the toxic behaviors exhibited by individuals irrespective of gender. Embracing a narrative that sees men as integral allies in the journey towards societal betterment will not only correct misconceptions but also promote a truly inclusive approach to resolving the complex issues facing today's world.

The continuous berating of traditional masculinity without a balanced understanding of its values can create a void. Many men feel lost, unsure of their place or value in today's rapidly changing world. Masculinity is not inherently toxic. Like femininity, it has its strengths and weaknesses. But painting it with a broad brush of negativity does a disservice to men and society at large. If we continue on this path, where masculinity is diminished without offering a clear, positive direction, we risk a future where men are disenfranchised, disengaged, and disillusioned.

In a society that thrives on balance, it's crucial that we address men's issues with the same fervor and women's. By understanding and supporting the well-being of men, we ensure a balanced, harmonious future for all. Ignoring these issues or worse, belittling them, will have profound repercussions for our collective future. It's a future where families may suffer, communities could disintegrate, and societal structures might collapse. In the end, everyone, irrespective of gender, stands to lose.

Embracing Masculinity: A Call to Men - A Personal Message

Men, now is the time to stand tall and claim your masculinity with pride, with no need for apologies. The essence of being a man isn't defined by the brute force of dominance, nor by the suppression of emotion. It's a balance, a harmonious blend of assertiveness and kindness, leadership with empathy, strength coupled with sensitivity. In a world where the traditional roles of men are often scrutinized or criticized, your voice, your perspective, is not just necessary—it's vital. Rise and speak with courage against the injustices, challenge the stereotypes that confine not only you but also those around you.

Turn away from the passive, the digital distractions that keep you from the richness of life. Instead, step into the arena of your community, engage with the physical world, and let your presence be felt, not just seen. Physical activity, social engagement, these are not mere pastimes; they are the expressions of your commitment to yourself, to your community. Confidence, leadership—these aren't just traits to be admired; they're the foundation upon which you build relationships, forge connections, and leave a legacy.

Let your life be a testament to your resolve, a beacon for those who feel lost in the noise of modern society. In a culture that too often plays the blame game, that wallows in victimhood, choose to break free. Your destiny is not written by the hands of others nor by the societal expectations that might seek to bind you. It's sculpted by your resilience, your unwavering grit, and the deep belief in what you can achieve.

Reject the mantle of victimhood, for it serves no purpose but to keep you down. Stand up, not just for yourself, but for the future generations of men who will look back and see your struggle as the foundation for their triumphs. Build your path, not with bitterness, but with purpose, with the understanding that each step you take forward is a step towards breaking down the barriers for all.

As you navigate this journey, hold fast to your convictions. In a world divided by noise, where narratives clash, be the calm, the steady hand. Recognize the humanity in everyone you meet, for beneath the labels and the stereotypes, we are all individuals with stories, hopes, and dreams. Your growth, your journey towards becoming the best version of yourself, is not just personal—it's inspirational, a guiding light for those who walk the path behind you.

Remember, you are part of a brotherhood, a movement of men who refuse to be defined by the narratives of the past or the present. Your courage to redefine masculinity, to embrace all its facets with integrity and love, this is not just your victory; it's a beacon for broader change. Be the role model, the mentor, the guide that shows others the true power of masculinity lies not in oppression but in empowerment, not in division but in unity, not just in survival but in thriving.

Let education, let life itself, be your canvas where you paint the picture of masculinity not as a restrictive role but as a dynamic, evolving identity. Foster environments where young boys can see in you, not just a man, but the potential of what they can become—a person of depth, of compassion, of strength, of integrity.

Men, this is your call to arms, not for war, but for peace; not for dominance, but for partnership; not for silence, but for dialogue. Embrace your masculinity, not as a shield to hide behind, but as a sword to carve out a place in the world where you, and all men, can stand with heads held high, hearts open wide, and eyes looking forward to a future where masculinity is celebrated for its contributions, its love, its leadership, and its endless capacity for growth.

A Call to Women: Championing True Equality and Celebrating Masculinity

Dear women, in our journey toward genuine equality and justice, it is vital to recognize the narratives that have swayed far from the middle, pushing many to view masculinity through a lens tinted with suspicion and negativity. As we stand together on the frontlines of societal advancement, it's crucial to remember the power of unity and the strength that comes from supporting each other, irrespective of gender.

The modern-day crusade to dismantle what is often termed the 'patriarchy' has unfortunately veered into a zone where the qualities that define men are often dismissed wholesale. This narrative not only undermines the true essence of equality but also forgets the countless positive impacts men have made and continue to make in our world. As partners, fathers, and leaders, men play irreplaceable roles that deserve recognition and appreciation, not blanket criticism.

We must steer our collective focus towards an equality that uplifts all, not one that seeks to tear down half of us. The notion that men are responsible for all societal ills is not only unconstructive but deeply harmful. It propagates division rather than understanding, and alienation over alliance.

By recognizing the good in men, we foster an environment where true equality is not just a goal but a reality.

Let us then, with open hearts and minds, reject the over-simplifications that have plagued discussions about gender. Men, like women, are not monolithic; they embody a spectrum of virtues and vices, strengths, and struggles. Acknowledging this fact is the first step towards dismantling the generalized accusations that serve only to deepen the gender divide.

It is time to embrace a narrative that recognizes the challenges men face—challenges like mental health issues, societal pressure to conform to outdated standards, and the need for positive role models. Addressing these issues with the same passion we advocate for women's issues will not only bring balance to our discourse but will also heal and strengthen our communities.

Moreover, as we advocate for support systems that address women's needs, let us also build and fortify the structures that support men. Initiatives to help men cope with the pressures of modern life, encourage healthy expressions of emotion, and celebrate their positive contributions to society are not just beneficial but necessary for a holistic societal health.

In fostering this balanced dialogue, we encourage men to be proud of their masculinity, not as a means of domination but as a source of strength to be channeled positively. Masculinity that embodies responsibility, empathy, and courage is something to be celebrated, not feared or shunned.

A Lighthearted Plea to Women: The Case for Keeping Masculinity Around

Ladies, let's talk men. Not just any men, but those sturdy, dependable sorts who have traditionally been known to take the bull by the horns, not run from them. Now, we understand that the modern narrative has been tough on these guys. Turn on the TV and you might find that the bumbling dad or the clueless husband has replaced the strong, silent types of yesteryear. But let's pause for a moment and ask ourselves: when the chips are down and the Wi-Fi is out, who do we really want by our side?

Imagine this: the power's gone, there's a spider in the bathtub, and the only thing standing between you and total anarchy is someone who's read more self-help books than manuals on how to change a tire. It's a quirky scenario, but it underscores a point—confidence and resilience are kind of sexy, aren't they?

We jest, of course, but beneath this playful banter lies a serious note. The allure of a man who exudes confidence and competence isn't just the stuff of romance novels; it's rooted in a very real desire for security and partnership. Sure, vulnerability is important, and yes, we all adore a man who can share his feelings over a glass of wine. But let's not undervalue the type who can share those feelings while also figuring out why the furnace is making that weird noise and who can take charge during an emergency.

It seems, however, that the pendulum has swung a bit too far from the statuesque hero towards the overly subdued, leading to a peculiar form of male representation in media and culture. Men, once the revered pillars in stories of valor and virtue, now often play the fool, with their once-celebrated masculinity left hanging in the wardrobe next to their granddad's fedora—outdated and out of style.

But, dear ladies, before we toast to the downfall of the dashing, let's consider the consequences. In our zeal to level the playing field, we must be wary of bulldozing the very qualities that many of us find appealing. Do we really want to edge out the bold, the brave, and the gallant for a world where no one is prepared to deal with a flat tire on a rainy night?

So, as we continue striving for equality, let's not consign traditional masculinity to the relics of history. Instead, let's encourage our men to be both strong and easy-going, assertive and understanding, romantic and real. After all, a man who can navigate both a crisis and a conversation about his feelings? Now, that's a hero worth holding onto.

Here's a 5-step practical plan for society to address and reverse the trend of the downfall of men:

Step 1: Education Reform

- **Introduce Gender-Inclusive Curriculum:** Revise educational content to include narratives of positive male role models and contributions, similar to how female achievements are highlighted. This should promote a balanced view of gender roles and achievements.

- **Tailored Educational Support:** Recognize that boys and girls might have different learning styles and needs. Implement programs that offer tailored support to boys in areas where they traditionally lag, such as reading and emotional intelligence.

Step 2: Media and Cultural Representation

- **Encourage Varied Portrayals:** Advocate for media outlets to diversify their portrayal of men, moving away from stereotypes of incompetence or aggression towards more nuanced, positive characters. This could involve discussions with media creators, awards for positive male representation, and public campaigns highlighting exemplary male figures.

- **Promote Positive Masculinity:** Use public service announcements, social media campaigns, and educational programs to promote what positive masculinity looks like, emphasizing leadership, empathy, and community involvement.

Step 3: Workplace and Career Development

- **Mentorship Programs:** Establish mentorship programs in schools and workplaces that connect young men with successful mentors. These programs should focus on career guidance, personal development, and navigating modern societal expectations.

- **Equitable Work Policies:** Encourage companies to review their policies to ensure they are not inadvertently biased against men in areas like parental leave, flexible working hours, or career advancement opportunities.

Step 4: Mental Health Initiatives

- **Accessible Mental Health Services:** Increase funding and accessibility to mental health services specifically targeted at men, recognizing the unique challenges they face, such as higher suicide rates and societal pressure to 'man up'.

- **Awareness Campaigns:** Launch campaigns aimed at reducing the stigma around men seeking help for mental health issues. Include educational workshops on emotional expression and resilience.

Step 5: Community and Social Engagement

- **Men's Groups:** Support the formation of community groups where men can discuss issues, share experiences, and support each other. These groups could range from hobby clubs to community service organizations.

- **Encourage Community Involvement:** Promote and facilitate men's participation in community activities to broaden their perspective, and to gain skills and for enjoyment.

- Implementing these steps requires a collaborative effort between governments, educational institutions, media, and community leaders. It's about fostering a culture where men can thrive without the constraints of outdated or harmful stereotypes, and where their contributions are recognized and valued as integral to society's well-being. By doing so, we not only uplift men but also strengthen the fabric of our communities, promoting equality and mutual respect across all genders.

The Safety Dance: A Wry Look at the Western Desire for Comfort Over Courage

- **Men's Groups:** Support the formation of community groups where men can discuss issues, share experiences, and support each other. These groups could range from hobby clubs to community service organizations.

- **Encourage Community Involvement:** Promote and facilitate men's participation in community activities to broaden their perspective, and to gain skills and for enjoyment.

- Implementing these steps requires a collaborative effort between governments, educational institutions, media, and community leaders. It's about fostering a culture where men can thrive without the constraints of outdated or harmful stereotypes, and where their contributions are recognized and valued as integral to society's well-being. By doing so, we not only uplift men but also strengthen the fabric of our communities, promoting equality and mutual respect across all genders.

Ah, the West—land of the free, home of the brave, and lately, the playground of the overly cautious. Gone are the days when children roamed the neighborhood until the streetlights came on. Today, they're shepherded from one supervised playdate to another, driven to school despite living blocks away, all in the name of safety. Are we raising children or bonsai trees—carefully pruned and protected from the wildness of nature?

This ever-increasing bubble wrap approach to life doesn't stop with child-rearing. Oh no, it extends to every corner of our lives. Remember when playgrounds were battlegrounds for resilience? Those towering metal slides that were scorching hot in the summer and the monkey bars proudly displaying the battle scars of childhood? Now, they are cushioned by rubber, and any equipment deemed 'too risky' has been phased out. It's as if we've decided that the only way to protect our children is to prevent any risk at all, forgetting that resilience is forged in the fires of scraped knees and sunny day squabbles.

And let's talk about our borders, shall we? Our forefathers might have braved the vast unknown for a taste of freedom, but today, we swing our gates wide open, not out of a pioneering spirit of adventure and growth, but from a pathological altruism that insists on helping everyone at once, even at the expense of reasonable caution.

In a world where every child gets a trophy, we have to wonder, are we celebrating mediocrity? Are we becoming so obsessed with not offending that we risk the vigor and vitality that come from healthy competition and striving for excellence? Where is the chapter in the parenting manual about teaching our kids to lose gracefully or the importance of standing up after a fall?

If we keep this up, the future memoirs of our civilization might just be titled "*How the West Was Mild.*" A catchy title for sure, and it would fly off the shelves in the humor section, sandwiched between books on knitting and vegan cookbooks. But is that the legacy we aspire to? A legacy of caution tapes and sanitized adventures?

To those nodding along, worrying about the emasculation of our culture through overprotection and under-exposure to the ruggedness of life, I propose a return to the essentials. Let's teach our children to climb trees, ride bikes, or at least walk to school. Let's open our doors to the world, but not without a sensible bouncer at the gate. And for heaven's sake, let's put the adventure back in the adventure playground!

For more on forging resilience and combating the safe-space culture overwhelming our society, check out my book, *Resisting the Tide: A Youth's Guide to Thriving Amidst Woke Culture.* It's packed with strategies to help the next generation navigate these padded playgrounds of life without losing their grit. After all, life isn't about avoiding the storm; it's about learning to dance in the rain—preferably not under an umbrella the whole time.

From Pathological Altruism to Rational Compassion

In the West, we find ourselves in an era of pathological altruism, where we house illegal immigrants at taxpayers' expense while our most vulnerable citizens languish in poverty. We send vast sums abroad to finance wars, while our own cities decay from neglect. This trend seems to stem from a form of cultural self-hatred that has become deeply ingrained in our media and educational narratives. We are continually taught about the purported evils of the West, often with little balance or perspective.

From my clinical experience, I have observed individuals who suffer from self-hatred. They often have an unconscious drive towards self-destruction and self-sabotage, a pattern distressingly mirrored in Western policies and cultural attitudes today. There is a dire need for a rebalancing act—where we prioritize our own societal needs without diminishing our capacity for community and compassion within the global world.

This necessary shift calls for embracing a framework that I perceive as more traditionally masculine—one that values directness, rationality, and a pragmatic approach to empathy. Instead of succumbing to excessive empathy and pathological altruism, which seem to be driving the West towards self-destruction, we must champion an approach rooted in common sense. We need to ensure our own societal well-being first, making us better equipped to genuinely help others. This is not about diminishing compassion but about channeling it in ways that strengthen rather than undermine our societal foundations.

QUESTIONING CLIMATE DOGMAS WITHOUT GETTING BURNED

As we navigate through the intricacies of society and the roles we play within it, our journey brings us to a crucial and ubiquitous aspect of our lives—our relationship with the Earth. This relationship, marked by both reverence and exploitation, has been dominated by an increasingly polarized discourse: the climate dogma. It is a narrative fraught with dire predictions and urgent calls for drastic measures, often leaving little room for dissent or discussion.

Climate dogma, as it stands today, paints a picture of impending doom, a scenario where the Earth teeters on the brink of a cataclysmic breakdown, primarily due to human activity. This narrative is so pervasive that to question its premises is often seen as heretical, a denial of science itself. Yet, it is in the spirit of true scientific inquiry that we must approach this topic—not as unquestionable dogma but as a complex, evolving subject that demands critical thinking and open dialogue.

Moreover, questioning the climate dogma allows us to explore a wider range of solutions, some of which may be sidelined in the mainstream discourse. It opens the door to innovative technologies, alternative energy sources, and novel approaches to carbon capture and sequestration. It also invites us to look critically at the economic and political interests that shape the climate conversation, ensuring that policies are not only environmentally sound but also socially equitable.

This section serves as a beacon through the dense fog of radical climate discourse. Here, I undertake a journey similar to those in Unicornia, where we challenge prevailing dogmas, confront uncomfortable truths, and seek deeper understanding within the intricate realm of ecological stewardship. Braving the potential backlash from challenging mainstream narratives, this section provides a refuge for the inquisitive mind.

Encouraging rigorous scrutiny and open dialogue, I invite you to traverse the lush landscapes of eco-awareness. Armed with an open heart and a discerning eye, we delve into environmental debates that demand more than passive acceptance but thoughtful engagement. Join me in this critical examination, where curiosity leads the way in our ongoing quest for truth.

In the grand theatrical production that is modern society's response to climate change, there exists a script so densely packed with hyperbole and doom-laden prophecy that even the ancient oracles would advise a rewrite for clarity's sake. This guide, dear reader, is your annotated playbook to navigating the tempestuous seas of climate discourse, where hyperbole is the prevailing wind, and reason often finds itself capsized by the sheer force of alarmist rhetoric. As we embark on this journey, let us arm ourselves with the twin shields of satire and sobriety, for the path ahead is fraught with both absurdity and peril.

The world, it seems, has become a stage where every actor vies for the spotlight, delivering lines of impending disaster with the fervor of a Shakespearean tragedy. "The end is nigh!" cry the prophets of climate doom, casting carbon as the villain in a saga that spans the globe. But in the rush to avert this scripted apocalypse, we risk entangling ourselves in a plot so convoluted that the original message of environmental stewardship is lost in translation. This guide seeks to untangle these narratives, offering a beacon of levity in a dialogue that often veers into the melodramatic.

Through the lens of satire, we'll explore the caricatures and contradictions that populate the climate change conversation, from the eco-warriors who demand emission cuts while jet-setting across the skies, to the paradox of advocating for drastic measures that disproportionately harm those they aim to protect. Our journey will reveal the comedy and tragedy interwoven in the fabric of the environmental movement, highlighting the need for a script revision that champions both the planet's health and humanity's.

Yet, as we navigate this landscape of extremes, it becomes evident that the stakes are no laughing matter. The dangers of climate change hyperbole are real and the hysteria and misinformation that often accompany the discourse serve to alienate, rather than unite. This guide, therefore, serves a dual purpose: to cut through the noise with humor, and to ground the conversation in a more measured, thoughtful examination of our collective path forward.

As the final act approaches, our narrative will shift from the satirical to the sincere, posing serious questions and reflections on how society can address the challenges of climate change without succumbing to the pitfalls of extremism. This is not just a guide to surviving the hyperbolic storm but a call to action for all who seek a balanced, informed approach to one of the most pressing issues of our time.

The need for this guide has never been more acute. In an era where information is abundant, yet wisdom is scarce, discerning the signal from the noise requires a discerning eye and a critical mind. Through satire, we pierce the veil of doom, and with earnest inquiry, we seek solutions that are both pragmatic and equitable. This is the essence of our quest: to navigate the treacherous waters of climate discourse with a compass calibrated by reason, and a healthy dose of humor.

From Ice Age to Climate Change: A Journey Through Environmental Paradigms

Growing up in the 1970s, my childhood was punctuated by episodes of "In Search Of," narrated by the late, great Leonard Nimoy. Among the myriad of mysteries and phenomena explored on the show, one topic that stood out was the looming threat of an impending ice age. This notion, widely discussed during that decade, cast a shadow of concern over the public consciousness, including my own youthful mind. While the complexities of climate science were far beyond my understanding as a child, the idea of the Earth cooling to potentially catastrophic levels was enough to instill a sense of unease. Yet, in an era devoid of social media's omnipresence, life marched on with a semblance of normalcy. I went to school, engaged in the quintessential Canadian pastimes of hockey and football, and the fear of a new ice age gradually receded into the background of my everyday life.

Fast forward to the mid-1980s, during my high school years, and the narrative had dramatically shifted. The conversation was no longer about global cooling but had instead taken a 180-degree turn to global warming and the greenhouse effect. This abrupt change in the climate discourse sparked a memory of the "In Search Of" episode, prompting me to question my teacher about the fate of the once-feared global cooling phenomenon. My inquiry was met with confusion, an indication of the evolving and often perplexing nature of climate science communication at the time.

As the years progressed, new environmental concerns emerged, including acid rain, a hole in the ozone layer, and a steady increase in global temperatures. Eventually, the term "global warming" broadened into "climate change," a phrase that seemed to encapsulate the myriad ways our planet's climate could be shifting. This evolution of terminology, from global cooling to climate change left me wondering why this shift occurred.

I must clarify; I acknowledge the reality of global warming. Yet, the introduction of "climate change" into our lexicon marks a pivotal moment in the environmental dialogue. The genius—or perhaps the cunning—of "climate change" lies in its catch-all nature, a term so encompassing that any variation in weather patterns or climate anomalies can be attributed to it. Excessive rain, drought, heatwaves, or un-seasonable cold, all fall under the umbrella of climate change, a term that, by its very definition, cannot be disproven.

This broad application of "climate change" has not only influenced scientific discourse but has permeated every aspect of societal conversation, from policy initiatives to everyday discussions. It has become a scapegoat for a wide array of environmental issues, with calls to dramatically alter our way of life in response to this all-encompassing threat. The push for draconian measures, fueled by social media and certain factions within the environmental movement, has led to debates over the balance between safeguarding our environment and preserving the freedoms and norms of Western civilization.

In an age where the line between environmental activism and absurdist theater increasingly blurs, one can't help but marvel at the lengths to which many elements of the environmental movement will go to save the planet—or, more accurately, to save us from ourselves. As I embark on this exploration, I wield satire, humor, and sarcasm not as mere literary devices, but as tools to excavate the underlying truths buried beneath the surface of good intentions gone awry.

Picture, if you will, a world meticulously engineered by the most ardent of eco-warriors. In this verdant paradise, cows are banished to the annals of history for their scandalous methane indiscretions, leaving dairy aficionados worldwide in a state of existential crisis. Automobiles, those roaring beasts of burden, are relegated to museum exhibits, as humanity reverts to a nomadic lifestyle, albeit with the added flair of electric scooters (because, let's face it, walking is so last millennium).

But why stop at mere transportation and agriculture? In a bold stroke of genius, these eco-visionaries propose a ban on human respiration—after all, every exhalation is a carbon emission. With tongue firmly in cheek, we jest at these hyperbolic solutions, yet they serve a crucial purpose: to highlight the absurdity that sometimes infiltrates the discourse on environmental protection, obscuring practical solutions with a veil of well-meaning zealotry.

Yet, as we stand at this crossroads, we must choose our path wisely. The journey ahead requires us to navigate the delicate balance between environmental stewardship and the preservation of individual liberties. It demands of us a vision that is both ambitious and grounded, one that champions innovation and inclusivity over restriction and dogma.

In a world teeming with the unbridled joy of artistic freedom and the boundless benefits of restricting personal liberties for the greater good, let's take a moment to celebrate the innovative strides we're making towards ensuring our planet's health by, well, slightly unconventional means. Who knew that the path to environmental salvation was paved with the crushed dreams of cultural heritage and individual freedoms? Let's dive into this satirical exploration with all the sarcasm and wit we can muster.

THE ART OF SACRIFICE: A TOAST TO ENVIRONMENTAL ZEALOTS

Ah, the gallant environmental movement, our valiant hero donned in armor crafted from the finest recycled materials, bravely stumbling on the drawstrings of its sustainably sourced hemp shoes. In its noble quest to rescue Mother Earth from the clutches of humanity's folly, it appears a few of its more, shall we say, fervent disciples, notably the avant-garde troupe known as Just Stop Oil, have unearthed a revolutionary tactic: the strategic disruption of the masses' mundane existence, with the occasional side effect of sidelining that irksome ambulance. Because, in the grand cosmic ledger, what are a few human inconveniences against the backdrop of planetary salvation?

Picture, if you will, the audacity of blocking thoroughfares, those asphalt rivers of communal life, transforming rush hour into a static tableau of existential despair. And for what? To etch into our collective consciousness the incontrovertible truth that trees, indeed, possess a higher existential value than, say, someone's timely access to medical care. This, my friends, is the sort of enlightenment that only comes from standing, sign in hand, in the middle of a highway, basking in the chorus of honks and the fragrance of exhaust fumes—a small price to pay for the greater good.

But why stop at mere traffic disruptions? The movement, in its infinite wisdom, has taken to assaulting our cultural institutions, splattering masterpieces of art with substances less savory, in acts of defiance so bold, they make Banksy's escapades seem like child's play. For what better way to underscore the importance of clean air than by defacing the creations of master works of Art? It's a message as clear as the smog-free sky we're all aiming for: Art, schmart. If it doesn't photosynthesize, it's expendable.

Indeed, this cadre of eco-warriors, armed with the moral high ground and a penchant for public spectacle, has redefined activism for the modern age. Gone are the days of quaint sit-ins and peaceful marches. No, in the era of virality, nothing less than the complete upheaval of daily life will suffice to capture the fleeting attention of the public eye. "Disrupt, therefore we are," seems to be the new mantra, chanted with the fervor of a revivalist choir, albeit one dressed in upcycled garments and biodegradable footwear.

Let us pause, however, to ponder the sheer genius of this approach. In a stroke of unparalleled strategic mastery, they've managed to alienate the very populace they seek to enlighten, transforming potential allies into adversaries bewildered by the correlation between artistic vandalism and environmental advocacy.

Amidst this carnival of chaos, one can't help but marvel at the movement's dedication to its cause, a commitment so profound it transcends the boundaries of reason and good taste. It's as if they've taken to heart the old adage, "You have to break a few eggs to make an omelet," applying it with a liberality that would make even the most hardened chef blush. After all, what's a smattering of egg on the face of society if it means saving the planet?

In the final analysis, as we navigate the debris field of disrupted lives and besmirched artworks, we must concede a grudging admiration for the environmental movement's chutzpah. For it takes a special brand of courage to proclaim, amidst the cacophony of modern life's discontents, that the road to salvation is paved with inconveniences, and that the penultimate act of reverence for our planet involves a can of spray paint and a disregard for cultural heritage. So here's to clean air, at any cost. May the trees (and only the trees) stand in testament to our folly.

The Great Green Leap Forward: Sacrificing the Few for the Many

Ah, the grand odyssey towards green technology, where the roadmap is as clear as mud and the tolls are priced for the gods. It's a journey of enlightenment, one where the average Joe and Jane are invited to leap into the future—provided, of course, they can pony up the green to go green. Retrofitting homes, purchasing electric vehicles, and adopting renewable energy sources are presented as the keys to the kingdom of sustainability, small potatoes for the proletariat, surely.

But, dear peasants, fear not the financial abyss that gapes before you. The transition to a greener tomorrow is as easy as pie—a pie that's been locked in a safe, at the top of a tree, guarded by a fire-breathing dragon. Want to reduce your carbon footprint? Simply invest in solar panels for the mere cost of your soul and a couple of firstborns. Fancy an electric vehicle? They're practically giving them away, for the low, low price of your left kidney and perhaps a pledge of eternal allegiance to the cult of Tesla. And let's address the elephant in the room, or rather, the diamond-encrusted unicorn: the notion that the transition to green technology might, just might, disproportionately benefit those whose wallets are as thick as the plot of an eco-thriller. But worry not, for this is merely the natural order of things. The environmental movement, in its wise oversight, has decreed that sustainability is, indeed, a privilege reserved for the elite. Equality in the green revolution is achieved by ensuring that everyone has an equal opportunity to gaze longingly at the greener grass on the other side, provided they can afford the binoculars to see it.

In this light, the notion that 9.2% of the world lives in extreme poverty, subsisting on less than $1.90 a day, emerges not just as a statistic, but as a stark reminder of the grand canyon between the eco-haves and the eco-have-nots. This figure, while a testament to the strides made in reducing global poverty, also highlights the paradoxical luxury of environmental stewardship—a luxury that remains elusive for the many who are preoccupied with the daily grind of survival, far removed from the dilemmas of carbon footprints and organic produce.

The brilliance of this approach cannot be overstated. By making green technology an exclusive club, we ensure that its members are truly committed to the cause—so committed that they're willing to pay a premium for the privilege of moral superiority. After all, nothing says "I care about the planet" quite like a rooftop decked in solar panels that cost more than a small island.

This strategy also serves as a masterful stroke of social engineering, subtly reinforcing the idea that environmental responsibility is not a universal burden, but a luxury good. Like fine wine, designer fashion, and private education, a clean conscience is now something to be flaunted, not shared.

"Look at me," it whispers from the driveways of the affluent, "I'm saving the world, one tax-deductible donation at a time."

But let us not despair, for the environmental movement is nothing if not inclusive in its exclusivity. It extends a hand to the common folk, inviting them to participate in this noble crusade by adopting sustainable practices within their means—like recycling their plastics, composting their leftovers, and knitting their own clothes from the hair of organic, grass-fed yaks.

In the end, as we march arm in arm (but not too close, lest the unwashed masses tarnish the biodegradable fabric of the green elite's garments), we must remember that sustainability is not just a goal; it's a lifestyle. A lifestyle that is accessible to all who are willing to pay the price of admission. So, rally forth, ye eco-warriors of means, and lead the way into a greener, more exclusive future. For in the grand theatre of environmental salvation, it is the affluent who are cast as the heroes, lighting the path with their LED torches, while the rest of us follow in the dark, hoping to catch a glimmer of the spotlight, all the while pondering the irony that, for those living on less than $1.90 a day, the future painted green is but a distant dream, blurred by the more immediate hues of survival and daily bread.

THE LEADERSHIP PARADOX: DO AS I SAY, NOT AS I DO

Ah, the illustrious crusaders of our time, jet-setting across the blue marble, from summit to summit, in their quest to save us all from the impending doom of our own carbon excess. Bill Gates, Al Gore, and their merry band of eco-elites, soaring through the stratosphere, leaving contrails of wisdom in their wake. It's a spectacle of such grand irony; one can hardly resist the urge to stand and applaud their commitment to the cause.

Imagine, if you will, these titans of environmental advocacy, disembarking from their private jets, clothed in the fabric of moral superiority, ready to impart their sage advice on the masses huddled below. "Reduce your footprint," they proclaim, as the engines of their Gulfstreams cool in the background. "Embrace sustainability," they urge, moments before stepping into a motorcade of SUVs destined for the nearest five-star, eco-friendly resort. The message is clear: Do as I say, not as I fly.

Meanwhile, back on terra firma, the plebeians grapple with the trivialities of existence—poverty, hunger, homelessness. Such mundane concerns, however, are merely background noise to the grand symphony of environmental salvation being composed in the skies. Why worry about the roof over your head when the ozone layer is at stake? Why fret over your next meal when there are carbon credits to trade? The audacity of the common folk, to prioritize their immediate needs over the existential threat of climate change!

But fear not, for the elites have not forgotten about the little people. No, they are generous in their guidance, benevolent in their leadership. They understand that sacrifice is necessary, and they are more than willing to make those sacrifices on behalf of others. After all, what is the loss of a few thousand jobs in the energy sector compared to the satisfaction of hosting a successful climate conference in Bali or Davos?

And so, they continue to crisscross the globe, attending lavish fundraisers and penning op-eds from the comfort of their multi-million-dollar, environmentally sustainable mansions. They toast to the health of the planet with glasses of vintage wine, safe in the knowledge that their efforts will not go unnoticed by history. For who else but these champions of the Earth could navigate us through the perilous waters of climate change, with nothing but their unmatched expertise and a fleet of private jets?

Let us then, the unwashed masses, bow our heads in gratitude for the sacrifices these heroes are willing to make on our behalf. Let us humbly accept the draconian measures they impose from the comfort of their airborne palaces, for they know what is best for us. And when we lie awake at night, shivering in the dark because the energy grid can no longer support our needs, we can take solace in the fact that somewhere, at 30,000 feet, a billionaire is drafting the blueprint for our salvation.

In this grand narrative, poverty, hunger, and homelessness are but minor inconveniences, footnotes in the epic saga of environmental redemption. After all, what are the needs of the few compared to the survival of the planet? So, let us raise our reusable, bamboo cups to the sky and toast to our noble overlords. For in their wisdom, they have shown us the path to a greener, more equitable world—just as soon as they land.

Carbon Conundrums: Navigating the Green Maze with Empty Pockets

Let's dive into the whimsical world of carbon taxes, where the intentions are as green as an unripe tomato and the outcomes are as mixed as a thrift store blender. Here, in this eco-fantasy, we find that the burden of saving the Earth from turning into a giant barbecue falls squarely on the shoulders of those least equipped to bear it. Low-income individuals and families, already engaged in the Sisyphean task of making ends meet, are now expected to cheerfully contribute a bit more of their scant resources to the noble cause of carbon reduction. "Heat or eat?" becomes the new rallying cry, a choice as appetizing as a menu featuring boiled cardboard or toasted rubber.

But fear not, for the architects of these policies have assured us that this approach is the epitome of fairness. After all, what could be more equitable than a flat tax that impacts everyone equally, by which we mean disproportionately affecting those for whom a spike in gas prices means choosing between filling the tank and filling the fridge? It's a sort of Robin Hood strategy in reverse: rob from the poor, give to the... well, climate, and trust that the wealthy will toss a few carbon credits into the hat for good measure.

The brilliance of this strategy is that it adds a layer of moral superiority to everyday survival. Now, when a low-income family scrimps to pay their utility bill, they can bask in the warm glow of knowing they're contributing to the greater good, rather than cursing the darkness of a policy that effectively taxes them for existing. It's a win-win, if by winning, we mean patting ourselves on the back for our environmental consciousness while those impacted most struggle to adapt.

Amidst the shimmering facade of the environmental crusade, a stark contrast emerges, highlighting a chasm as wide and as deep as the mines from which we extract our precious lithium. The captains of this movement, steering the ship towards a greener horizon, often hail from realms of wealth and privilege so lofty, the air might indeed be cleaner up there. With resumes polished in the halls of Ivy League institutions and careers forged in the crucibles of high society, their crusade is as much a statement of fashion as it is of conviction.

This elite vanguard, adorned in the latest eco-conscious couture, seems to float above the mundane concerns of the average Earth dweller. Their campaigns, slick with the gloss of high-production values and celebrity endorsements, speak in the universal language of urgency yet often fail to translate into the dialects of practicality and accessibility that dominate the daily lives of billions. The message, while noble in its essence, is delivered from such heights that it occasionally gets lost in the thin air before reaching the ears of those on the ground.

The irony of this scenario is not lost on the observers: leaders who decry the carbon footprint of the masses while their own footprints stomp across the skies in private jets, leaving contrails of contradiction in their wake. Their exhortations for the world to embrace electric vehicles and renewable energy sources resonate with the hollow ring of a bell that has never known struggle, never felt the pang of energy poverty, nor faced the dilemma of choosing between warmth and food.

This lack of self-awareness, a blind spot as glaring as a solar flare, underscores a fundamental disconnect between the movement's champions and the realities of the majority of the planet. For those whose daily existence is a ballet of survival, the grand visions of a fully electrified future powered by the whispers of the wind and the caresses of the sun are as distant as a fable, as tangible as a mirage on the horizon.

As we forge ahead on this path, the leadership is urged to listen, question, and integrate multiple perspectives. This is crucial because, as history has shown us, nothing fosters equality and understanding quite like a roomful of extremely wealthy experts debating the best way to implement policies that will never affect them personally.

ELECTRIC DREAMS AND LITHIUM NIGHTMARES: THE HIGH SOCIETY OF GREEN ELITES

In the glittering world of environmental activism, where the air is cleaner at thirty thousand feet and electric cars glide silently through the streets of gated communities, a peculiar narrative unfolds. It's a tale of the rich and the privileged, the eco-crusaders who, from the comfort of their private jets and Tesla chariots, decree the future of sustainability for the rest of us mere mortals. These are the chosen few, anointed with the sacred task of saving Mother Earth, one luxury EV at a time, while gently chiding the unwashed masses for their carbon profligacy.

Ah, electric vehicles (EVs), those shiny beacons of hope, gliding through the smoggy reality of our fossil-fueled existence. They come to us as gleaming chariots of fire, promising salvation from the sins of combustion. Yet, beneath their polished exteriors lies a tangled web of inconvenient truths, spun from the very earth they vow to protect. The quest for lithium, that precious white gold powering our green dreams, unfolds as an epic saga, complete with environmental devastation, geopolitical intrigue, and the stark realization that we might just be trading one set of chains for another.

Picture, if you will, the lithium mines, where the earth is torn asunder not by the claws of some mythological beast but by the insatiable demand for battery-powered redemption. Here, in these blasted landscapes, the environmental toll of our green ambitions is laid bare, a stark reminder that every action has its equal and opposite reaction—especially when it involves ripping minerals from the bosom of Gaia herself.

And then there's the comedy of the rare earth metals, a term so misleading one might think it refers to a collection of exotic spices rather than the building blocks of our electrified future. These elements, as elusive as they are essential, have sparked a modern gold rush, igniting geopolitical tensions and raising the specter of resource wars—all in the name of saving the planet, of course.

But fear not, for our eco-warriors are nothing if not resourceful. With a wave of their magic wands (forged from sustainably sourced unicorn horns, no doubt), they assure us that technology will solve the problems technology has created. "More mining for sustainability," they proclaim, a mantra as paradoxical as it is perplexing. It's a vision of the future where the roads are paved with good intentions and lined with the debris of environmental paradoxes.

Amid this grand spectacle, the majority of the planet, including the one billion souls without electricity, are cast as unwitting extras in a drama they can scarcely afford to watch, let alone participate in. They are the silent chorus, their plight drowned out by the roar of electric motors and the incessant buzz of drone deliveries to the eco-elite's mountaintop retreats.

Yet, despite these challenges, the race towards electrification charges ahead, powered by the dual engines of optimism and denial. It's a race that promises to transform our world, to usher in an era of clean, green mobility—so long as we ignore the dirty, inconvenient truths lurking just beneath the surface.

So, let us strap in and enjoy the ride, for the road to a sustainable future is fraught with irony, paved with contradictions, and navigated by those with the means to never feel the bumps along the way. In this brave new world of electric dreams and lithium nightmares, one thing is clear: the journey to green might just be the most polluting part of all.

Eco-Anxiety and the Young: A Masterclass in Doom

Welcome to the modern world, where the noble art of instilling existential dread in our youth has been perfected to a T by the environmental movement. Ah, what a time to be alive, when every child's smartphone becomes a gateway to the end times, serving up a daily dose of global collapse with the morning cereal. It's as if the Brothers Grimm decided to dabble in climate science, weaving tales not of wicked witches and dark forests, but of a future where the Earth, quite literally, burns.

Let's face it, the mental landscape of today's youth doesn't need horror movies for thrills; they're living in one, courtesy of the latest environmental headlines. Our gift to the next generation? A planet on a precipice, a future fraught with disaster, all wrapped up with a bow made of melting ice caps. "Sweet dreams," we whisper, after bombarding them with stories of the coming eco-apocalypse. "May visions of carbon footprints dance in your heads."

The approach of our eco-evangelists is nothing short of revolutionary. Why gently nudge humanity towards change when you can terrify them into action? The Earth as a charred meatball, floating helplessly in space, is the bedtime story of choice, aimed at stirring up a fervent desire to save the planet. Of course, the method has the subtle nuance of a sledgehammer, akin to teaching a child to swim by tossing them into a raging ocean and yelling, "Flutter those arms, or else!"

And, oh, the results are spectacular. We've birthed a generation of eco-anxious warriors, for whom the sight of a plastic straw triggers visions of apocalypse, and a running car engine is akin to a personal affront to their future. The mental well-being of these young souls now mirrors the aftermath of a typhoon—chaotic, fragmented, and strewn with the flotsam and jetsam of what was supposed to be a worry-free youth.

But let's not sell ourselves short; this perpetual state of eco-panic is, surely, our crowning achievement. What better way to prepare the leaders of tomorrow than by immersing them in a relentless surge of despair today? After all, nothing fosters resilience like the constant reminder that the world might not be there when you're ready to inherit it.

In this grand scheme of things, making the youth anxious is, evidently, a stroke of genius. Why bother with the nuances of hope or the complexities of balanced discourse when the simplicity of doomsday narratives can offer such clear direction? "The world is ending; fix it," we say, passing the buck with the finesse of a relay racer in the Olympic finals.

Truly, the environmental movement has outdone itself, transforming eco-awareness into eco-anxiety with the elegance of a chainsaw carving a statue. The message is clear:

the future is bleak, and it's up to the kids to sort it out. After all, what better motivation could there be than the constant, gnawing fear that every breath might be contributing to the downfall of civilization as we know it?

So, here's to the environmental crusaders, the architects of anxiety, who have managed to turn the fight for a better world into a source of sleepless nights for an entire generation. May the echoes of their alarm bells ring in the ears of our youth, a siren song of despair to guide them through the troubled waters of the digital age. Because, in the end, if we can't offer them a solution, at least we can offer them a good scare.

THE GREEN NEW EXTREME: FROM CAPITALISM TO UNICORNIA

As we embark on this journey through the looking glass of environmental reform, where the calls for the abolition of conservatism and capitalism echo louder than a vegan dinner bell, it's worth recalling the lessons from my previous work, Unicornia Unveiled: The Teenage SJW's Dream and the West's Downfall. In this work, we explored a fantastical world where the impossible became the mundane, a place where dreams and reality danced in a kaleidoscope of absurdity. This narrative serves as a precursor to our current exploration, setting the stage for a world where the green new extreme isn't just a possibility—it's a blueprint for the future.

The Great Green Purge: In the newest chapter of the environmental saga, there's a growing chorus demanding the abolition of conservatism and capitalism, as if we were all participants in a grand game of societal Jenga. The idea, it seems, is to pull out these foundational blocks and see if the tower still stands. Spoiler alert: We're advised to stand clear of the collapse zone.

Capitalism's Swan Song: Imagine a world where capitalism is dethroned, replaced by an economy that values leaves and wind whispers as currency. The stock market of this brave new world trades in carbon credits and recycled dreams, where the richest individuals are those with the smallest carbon footprints. A utopian vision, surely, but with the minor downside of figuring out how to pay the bills with good intentions.

The Conservative Conundrum: The proposal to abolish conservatism has its own charm. After all, what's more exhilarating than reinventing the wheel while the car is still moving? The plan appears to be to replace tried and tested societal structures with... well, the details are still under wraps. But fear not, for the architects of this new age promise that blueprints will be revealed, just as soon as they figure out how to draw.

The Socialist Paradise: In the absence of capitalism, socialism stands tall, ready to distribute the wealth equally among all. Never mind that the wealth in question might soon consist solely of recycled cans and community gardens. But hey, at least everyone gets an equal share of the compost pile.

One World, One Government: The idea of a one-world government has never been more appealing, especially to those who find the notion of national sovereignty so passé. In this global village, decisions are made by a council of the most enlightened, who, by sheer coincidence, agree with everything the environmental movement says.

Klaus Schaub's Dream: Klaus Schaub, sitting in his eco-friendly tower, dreams of a world united under a single banner, where the WEF's every decree is embraced with the zeal of a Black Friday sale. In his vision, the world operates like a well-oiled machine, running on renewable energy and the collective will of the people (with just a hint of benevolent oversight).

The Carbon Credit Economy: With capitalism out of the picture, the new global currency is carbon credits. It's a simple system: breathe less, earn more. The wealthy can afford air, while the poor are left to reminisce about the days when oxygen was free. A fair system, no doubt, based entirely on one's carbon virtue.

The End of Private Ownership: Say goodbye to personal possessions, as everything now belongs to the community. Your car, your house, even your Netflix account—are all part of the collective good. Privacy is a concept as outdated as fossil fuels, and sharing is not just caring; it's the law.

The New Education System: In schools, history lessons on capitalism and conservatism are replaced with more useful subjects like Advanced Composting and the Mathematics of Carbon Offsetting. Children are raised not as individuals, but as future stewards of Mother Earth, their success measured not by grades, but by their ecological footprint.

The Fashion of the Future: In this new society, fashion takes a radical turn. Clothing made from anything other than recycled materials is considered a social faux pas. The height of luxury is a dress made from upcycled plastic bags, worn with a sense of moral superiority no designer brand could ever provide.

The Diet Dictates: Meat is a relic of the past. The new diet is strictly plant-based, supplemented by whatever insects one can forage. It's not just about being healthy; it's about making a statement with every bite. After all, nothing says "I care about the planet" quite like a mouthful of sustainably sourced grasshoppers.

The Final Frontier: In the end, this brave new world is marked by its uniformity. Every house is powered by solar panels and wind turbines, every meal is a testament to sustainability, and every conversation is an opportunity to remind each other of our moral superiority. And as for those who miss the old ways—conservatism, capitalism, personal freedom—they're gently reminded that nostalgia is just another form of pollution.

CRYSTAL BALLS AND CLIMATE CALLS: THE MISADVENTURES OF PREDICTING TOMORROW

Now, for a few moments, as a detour, let's embark on a journey through the nostalgic chronicles of climate prediction. Back in the still days of the first Earth Day in 1970, we were subjected to a veritable monsoon of predictions that promised a future of doom and gloom. Ah, the sweet naivety of the time! Our ever-reliable science forecasters confidently peered into their crystal balls and laid out for us a future where civilization would end in 30 years, famine conditions would be widespread, and mass starvation would become the order of the day. Quite the sunny prediction, wouldn't you say?

We begin our tale with our dear Harvard biologist George Wald who foresaw our civilization's end within 15 to 30 years. Well, I hate to break it to you George, but we're still chugging along, last time I checked.

Our friend Barry Commoner, a biologist, posited that we were in an environmental crisis threatening the very survival of the nation and the world as a suitable place for humans. Yet, here we are, still breathing and rather suitably inhabiting the world, I might add.

"Man must stop pollution and conserve his resources, not merely to enhance existence but to save the race from intolerable deterioration and possible extinction." A profound quote from The New York Times the day after the first Earth Day. Profound, yes. Accurate, not quite.

Then we have Paul Ehrlich, who declared in a rather daring fashion that by 1980, 100-200 million people per year would be starving to death. Ehrlich, buddy, maybe ease up on the doom-peddling a tad?

Ehrlich strikes again, this time with a prediction about the "Great Die-Off" between 1980 and 1989. While there were indeed a lot of hair metal bands in the '80s, I don't believe they accounted for quite that high a casualty rate.

And again, Ehrlich (a real ray of sunshine, this one) stating that "it is already too late to avoid mass starvation." We do appreciate the sentiment, Ehrlich, but it appears we've dodged that bullet too.

Peter Gunter, not to be outdone, chimed in with an apocalyptic timeline of his own. By the year 2000, according to Gunter, every region apart from Western Europe, North America, and Australia would be in famine. Dear Peter, have you checked the date recently?

Ah, Life magazine, who predicted that by 1985, we would all have to wear gas masks to survive air pollution and sunlight reaching earth would be reduced by half. I can confirm that I am indeed currently mask-free and catching some rays as I type this.

Ecologist Kenneth Watt declared that our land would soon become unusable due to nitrogen buildup. Well, Kenneth, gardens seem to be doing just fine!

Barry Commoner, making a return appearance, predicted that decaying organic pollutants would use up all the oxygen in America's rivers, causing fish to suffocate. Our fishy friends seem to be swimming along quite happily, last time I checked.

Paul Ehrlich yet again, this time predicting that smog would cause hundreds of thousands of deaths in just a few years. Thankfully, his prediction proved to be another case of smoggy vision.

Ehrlich further predicted that Americans born since 1946 would only have a life expectancy of 49 years. A bit off the mark, as the CDC currently reports the US life expectancy at 78.8 years.

Kenneth Watt, with his prediction that by the year 2000, we would run out of crude oil. News flash, Watt: my car still seems to be running just fine!

Harrison Brown from the National Academy of Sciences believed we'd run out of several crucial metals shortly after 2000. Seems like we found more reserves, or someone's been recycling really well!

Senator Gaylord Nelson claimed that in 25 years, between 75% and 80% of all species of living animals would be extinct. While might have some biodiversity issues, Nelson's prediction was a bit extreme.

Paul Ehrlich predicted that half of the organisms in tropical rainforests would vanish due to deforestation. A crucial issue indeed, but thankfully not as dire as Ehrlich feared.

Oh, and while we are on a roll, here are some more, so strap in, fellow travelers, because we're about to crank up the absurdity to new heights. Like a classic B-movie sequel that nobody asked for, we're delving into the mystical world of predictions gone hilariously awry. Let's embark on an odyssey of misfires that make a weatherman's inaccurate forecast look like a precise science.

1967: They saw 'Dire Famine By 1975'. Someone's crystal ball was clearly fogged by their overpriced latte.

1969: They swore 'Everyone Will Disappear In a Cloud Of Blue Steam By 1989'. Is that the latest vape trend I missed?

1970: The impending 'Ice Age By 2000'. Someone clearly mistook their freezer frost for a global phenomenon.

1970: America was meant to suffer 'Water Rationing By 1974 and Food Rationing By 1980'. My apartment pool and well-stocked fridge beg to differ.

1971: A 'New Ice Age Coming By 2020 or 2030'. Grab your parkas, folks. And maybe a calendar.

1972: They saw a 'New Ice Age By 2070'. At this point, even Ice Age movie franchise gave up.

1974: 'Space Satellites Show New Ice Age Coming Fast'. Apparently, space satellites can get frostbite, too.

1974: Another 'Ice Age'? This is getting colder than my ex's heart.

1974: Ozone Depletion a 'Great Peril to Life'. Ironically, my indoor plant is still flourishing.

1976: Scientific Consensus that Planet is Cooling, Famines imminent. Did they also predict the rise of air conditioning and food delivery apps?

And we're just getting started! We've got Acid Rain in 1980, Regional Droughts (that never happened) in 1990s, and the 2000 prophecy that 'Children Won't Know what Snow Is'. I guess Frosty the Snowman is just a figment of our imagination now.

Some of the greatest hits include the bold 1988 prediction that 'Maldive Islands will Be Underwater by 2018'. Last time I checked, the Maldives is still a top vacation spot, not a diving expedition. And don't get me started on 1989's declaration that 'New York City's West Side Highway Underwater by 2019'. Someone forgot to tell the commuters that.

The list of misfires continues to impress with the 2009 assertion that we have '50 Days to 'Save The Planet From Catastrophe'. Has anyone been counting?

Peppered throughout these misprognostications are numerous 'The End of Oil' warnings, starting from 1966's 'Oil Gone in Ten Years', to the 2002 forecast of 'Peak Oil in 2010'. At this point, I'm sure the oil industry feels like an underrated pop song that just won't stop topping the charts.

Finally, we wrap up with the superpowered warning of 2006: 'Super Hurricanes!' If only they had put as much energy into accurate predictions as they did into alliteration.

Here we are, decades later, still muddling through, without the cataclysmic dystopia that was promised. Was this a fluke, you ask? Or perhaps the result of our feverish efforts to combat these impending disasters? Well, consider this: an alarming amount of the predictions that have been made over the years have failed to come true. So many, in fact, that one might wonder if we're dealing with climate science or an assembly line of doom-themed fiction novels.

The hilarious aspect of these apocalyptic prophecies is that they cover an amusingly vast range of disasters. According to our climate soothsayers, we should have run out of oil, copper, lead, zinc, tin, gold, silver, and oh, even sunlight by now. The world should have gotten colder, and almost 80% of animal species should have become extinct. All that's missing is a fire-breathing dragon and a cursed ring!

But the saga of climate change doesn't end there. Today, we are still given stark warnings of the catastrophic consequences if we do not transition completely away from fossil fuels. Of course, it is entirely reasonable to suggest that Canada, with its meager 2% of global greenhouse gas emissions, cutting back will save the world while China keeps puffing out emissions like a chain-smoking dragon. Nothing screams sensible like that, right?

The curious reality is that models struggle to predict the path of a hurricane after it has formed, but we are to trust models to guide policies that have far-reaching consequences, years and even decades into the future.

It's imperative to approach this subject with a balanced perspective. While recognizing global warming, we must also consider the impacts of sweeping policy changes on developing nations, food supplies, and the world's poor and middle-class citizens.

In the grand cathedral of environmental discourse, where the stained glass windows depict not saints, but graphs of rising CO_2 levels and the pews are filled with the faithful clutching reusable water bottles, questioning the sacred texts of climate models is tantamount to blasphemy. "Doubt," whispers the high priest of the Church of Climate Change, "is the greatest sin." And so, we find ourselves navigating the treacherous waters of inquiry, where even the most benign question can brand you a heretic.

Let us ponder, brethren and sistren, upon the heretical musings that dare to disturb the divine equilibrium of our eco-dogma. "How," asks the trembling voice of reason, "can we, the anointed of the West, bask in the warm glow of our energy-efficient LED lights, and still gradually reduce our reliance on the dark oils that flow like the rivers of Hades, without sacrificing the sacred cows of our standard of living?" A gasp echoes through the congregation, for here lies the great paradox: to save the Earth, must we return to the dark ages, lighting our way with nothing but the bio-luminescence of righteous indignation?

And yet, the sermon continues, for there is a second question, one that delves deeper into the moral quagmire. "How," intones the voice, now emboldened by its own audacity, "can this holy crusade for sustainability elevate the plight of the most vulnerable, those for whom the concept of a 'carbon footprint' is as alien as the notion of 'disposable income'?" The faithful shift uncomfortably in their seats, made from sustainably harvested guilt, for this question strikes at the heart of their doctrine. Can the Church of Climate Change extend its benevolence to all corners of the Earth, or does its salvation come with a price tag only the affluent can afford?

The high priests and priestesses of the movement, robed in garments of recycled fabric, woven with threads of moral superiority, ponder these queries. "Fear not," they proclaim, "for our eco-theology is vast and our technologies miraculous. We shall have our organic cake and eat it too, powered by the winds of change and the sun's eternal grace." And so, the congregation is soothed, their faith restored by the promise of technological deus ex machinas yet to be unveiled.

But the heretic, exiled to the wilderness for daring to question, watches from afar. They know that the path to environmental salvation is strewn with the complexities of human need and the thorny underbrush of economic disparity. "Is it possible," they wonder, casting their gaze upon the starry sky, not yet obscured by the smog of industry, "to forge a future where the Earth is revered, humanity is uplifted, and the LED lights of progress illuminate a world that is truly sustainable?"

Only time will tell if the sacred scrolls of climate models and the gospel of green technology can answer these questions without casting us all into the fiery pits of eco-purgatory. Until then, we continue our pilgrimage, armed with nothing but hope, a slightly used compost bin, and the audacity to dream of a world where questioning the narrative doesn't get you burned at the metaphorical stake.

Moving Forward

As we pivot from the sharp edges of satire to the earnest corridors of history and current affairs, let's draw from the past to illuminate our path forward. Reflecting on the unforgettable brawl between the Flyers and Canadiens in 1976 not only offers a vivid tableau of confrontation and change but also serves as a poignant allegory for our present challenges within the environmental movement.

This historical moment, where courage and unity on the ice demonstrated their power to redefine the dynamics of hockey rivalry, mirrors the urgent need for a cohesive and intelligent response to the fringe elements of today's climate discourse. Just as the Canadiens found a way to counter the 'Broad Street Bullies,' we, too, must find our collective voice to navigate and mitigate the hyperbolic and sometimes draconian narratives surrounding environmental action.

In the annals of NHL history, the notorious pre-season clash between the Montreal Canadiens and the Philadelphia Flyers in September 1975, in Philadelphia, stands as a pivotal moment that reshaped the dynamics between these two storied franchises. This confrontation, steeped in the lore of hockey's most tumultuous era, marked a significant turning point, challenging the dominance of the Flyers' infamous "Broad Street Bullies" persona.

Scotty Bowman, the astute Canadiens' coach, weary of witnessing his team being muscled out of their game by the Flyers' intimidating tactics, decided it was time for a change. In a bold move, Bowman orchestrated a power play unit unlike any other, positioning Larry Robinson at center, flanked by Sean Shanahan and Glen Goldup, with the formidable duo of Pierre Bouchard and Rick Chartraw anchoring the defense. This strategic assembly of players signaled a clear message: the Canadiens would no longer be cowed by the Flyers.

The catalyst for the ensuing melee was none other than Doug Risebrough, a player known for his fierceness, who engaged in a fierce altercation with the Flyers' Bobby Clarke. The situation quickly escalated as Dave Schultz, one of the Flyers' most feared enforcers, leapt into the fray. Within moments, the ice was a tableau of chaos, with fights erupting across its surface.

What unfolded was an unequivocal display of dominance by the Canadiens, who, contrary to expectations, emerged victorious in almost every confrontation. The brawl was described by Montreal journalists as the most significant the Canadiens had participated in for over three decades, a testament to its ferocity and the statement it made.

The game itself, overshadowed by the brawl, was called off by the referee once order was ostensibly restored, with the Canadiens leading 6-2. However, the true outcome of that night extended far beyond the scoreline. This event forever altered the complexion of future encounters between the Canadiens and Flyers. No longer would the Canadiens submit to intimidation; they had proven themselves capable of matching and surpassing the Flyers' physicality.

This legendary brawl not only signified the end of the "Broad Street Bullies'" reign of terror but also heralded a new era of resilience and tenacity for the Canadiens. The Canadiens also captured the Stanley Cup the following spring and this ushered in a new era of hockey.

The notorious brawl between the Canadiens and the Flyers offers a compelling metaphor for the current state of the environmental movement. Much like the NHL teams that once fell victim to the intimidation tactics of the "Broad Street Bullies," most of us pedestrian earthlings and even some within the climate discourse find themselves overshadowed by the more aggressive, elitist factions of the environmental movement. These groups, wielding their influence much like the Flyers wielded their physical prowess, often push for measures that will cause devastation to the poor and vulnerable. However, the 1976 Canadiens showed us that courage and unity can triumph over brute force. In a similar vein, confronting the extreme elements within the climate movement requires a strategy not of physical retaliation, but of cohesive and effective messaging, alongside a shared voice willing to speak out.

It becomes imperative to scrutinize the implications of such actions and explore viable alternatives. Relying solely on the passive intellectual citation of studies insufficient in a landscape where certain factions seek to exert control over our lives and liberties.

If one believes that the lockdowns were mere anomalies, it is time to reconsider. The prospect of future climate lockdowns, burdensome taxes, and policies that disregard the plight of the most vulnerable under the banner of saving Mother Earth is not only plausible but increasingly likely. Proposals for an eco-friendly future, often come at the expense of those least able to bear the burden, casting a long shadow over the lives of the poor and vulnerable, while the elite navigate these changes unscathed, their lifestyles uninterrupted by the very policies they advocate.

The challenge, then, is not to retreat into silence but to forge a path forward that acknowledges environmental stewardship without succumbing to the allure of simple, yet harmful, solutions. It is about crafting a narrative that is grounded in reality, and sensitive to the needs of the global community. By adopting a stance that values dialogue over dictation and pragmatism over panic, we can begin to outline a course of action that is both sustainable and just.

Addressing the increasingly disruptive tactics employed by certain factions within the environmental movement requires a return to principles of responsibility and accountability. Let's consider a straightforward approach to those activists who choose to block roadways, vandalize artworks, and generally impede the daily lives of individuals simply trying to make a living. The solution could indeed be simple: such activities, when they cross the line into illegality, should be met with appropriate legal consequences, including jail time and fines. Rather than mere admonishments or temporary detainments, a clear and stern message must be sent. This approach necessitates a shift in how society and law enforcement view and handle acts of environmental extremism that disregard public order and personal rights.

Moreover, it's imperative for individuals to actively engage in their communities and on social media, voicing opposition to draconian measures, oppressive taxes, and actions that more resemble intimidation tactics than genuine activism. Drawing inspiration from the resilience and unity displayed by the 1976 Canadiens, who refused to be bullied into submission, we too can stand firm against forces that seek to impose their will without dialogue or democratic consent.

Yet, amidst these calls for action and accountability, a series of pressing questions looms large, questions that seem to echo without answer across the halls of power and the spaces where environmental discourse predominates. The queries are fundamental, touching on the very fabric of our society and the global community: What are the real-world implications of striving for net zero, particularly for those already hanging by a thread in the socio-economic tapestry? How will policies designed to radically alter our energy consumption affect those living in the remote, unforgiving climates of the world's northern reaches?

The concept of net zero, a term bandied about with increasing frequency, demands clarification and scrutiny. What does achieving this state entail, and at what cost? The impact of carbon taxes on the economically disadvantaged must be thoroughly examined, as must the practicality of a wholesale shift to electric vehicles in a world where a significant portion of the population lacks access to basic electricity.

The environmental movement, while quick to spotlight the transgressions of certain industries and nations, often remains conspicuously silent on the environmental footprints of the American military-industrial complex and China's burgeoning industrial sector. Moreover, the irony of environmental figureheads, who decry carbon emissions yet routinely jet off to elite gatherings like Davos, cannot be overlooked. Such contradictions undermine the credibility of the movement and highlight a disconnect between preached virtues and practiced behaviors.

Equally concerning is the toll that environmental alarmism is taking on the mental health of our youth. The narrative of impending doom, relentlessly hammered into young minds, fosters a sense of despair and helplessness rather than empowerment or hope. Parents and caregivers thus find themselves in a critical position to counterbalance this narrative, emphasizing the importance of environmental stewardship while also equipping children with the tools to critically assess the information presented to them, both in academic settings and in the media.

Moving forward, amidst the earnest corridors of history and current affairs, the pressing need to confront and call out the seductive allure of utopian environmental solutions becomes ever more crucial. The stark realities of implementing such utopian ideals—often marked by sweeping, grandiose plans detached from the practicalities of everyday life—demand our scrutiny and, when necessary, serious opposition. It's a call to arms for people from all walks of life to engage in a critical dialogue, shedding light on the potential pitfalls and consequences of these idealistic ventures.

Utopianism in the environmental movement often manifests as a pursuit of an immaculate, perfectly sustainable world, free from the complexities and trade-offs that characterize our current struggle for environmental stewardship. This vision frequently overlooks the intricate balance required to navigate the socioeconomic landscapes that define our global community. The allure of such utopian dreams can, paradoxically, lead us down a path fraught with unintended consequences—where the cure prescribed becomes more debilitating than the ailment it sought to remedy.

As we engage with these utopian visions, it becomes evident that a nuanced, multifaceted approach to environmental challenges is not just preferable but essential. The experiences of nations that have pursued radical environmental agendas without due consideration of economic and social stability serve as stark reminders of the need for pragmatism in our approach to environmental policy and action. The tale of Sri Lanka's organic farming debacle is but one example of good intentions leading to disastrous outcomes when the complex realities of agricultural and economic systems are ignored in favor of an overly simplistic, utopian vision.

This moment in history calls for a resurgence of common sense—a rekindling of the pragmatic spirit that seeks sustainable solutions grounded in scientific rigor and , economic viability, It's a clarion call for individuals, communities, and nations to engage in a constructive critique of environmental utopianism, recognizing that the path to a more sustainable future is paved with incremental changes, technological innovation, and, most importantly, a deep respect for the needs and circumstances of people around the globe, especially the disadvantaged.

The discourse surrounding environmental action must transcend the binary of utopian idealism versus nihilistic inaction. Instead, it should embrace a spectrum of solutions that acknowledge the complexity of the challenges we face. This involves a willingness to question and critique, even as we advocate for change. It means calling out policies and practices that risk exacerbating the very problems they aim to solve or impose undue burdens on those least able to bear them.

In recognizing the complexity of our environmental challenges, it is imperative to address a critical aspect of our current energy landscape: the role of fossil fuels. Despite the push towards renewable energy sources, **the reality is that fossil fuels are not going away anytime soon.** This acknowledgment does not stem from a lack of ambition or commitment to environmental stewardship but from an understanding of the practical limitations and current global dependency on fossil fuels for energy, manufacturing, transportation, and more.

A balanced approach to environmental policy and energy transition is crucial. This approach must take into account the technological, economic, and societal challenges of abruptly moving away from fossil fuels. It involves investing in and scaling up renewable energy sources while simultaneously improving the efficiency and reducing the emissions of existing fossil fuel technologies. Such a strategy recognizes the importance of energy security, economic stability, and the need to support communities that currently depend on the fossil fuel industry.

Moreover, this balanced approach calls for realistic timelines for the energy transition, acknowledging that different regions and countries are at various stages of development and have differing capabilities for adopting renewable energy. It requires international cooperation and support for developing nations in their energy transition efforts, ensuring that the shift towards a more sustainable future is equitable and just.

Incorporating the continued role of fossil fuels into our vision of a sustainable future also means embracing innovations like carbon capture and storage (CCS) technologies, which can mitigate the impact of remaining fossil fuel use. It's about finding ways to make the transition as smooth and efficient as possible, without sacrificing the livelihoods of millions or destabilizing global economies.

Ultimately, a balanced approach towards our energy future and environmental stewardship acknowledges the complexities of the world we live in. It champions a pragmatic path forward that leverages all available technologies and strategies to reduce our environmental footprint. By embracing a multifaceted and inclusive approach, we can work towards a sustainable future without overlooking the practical realities of our current global energy system. This pragmatic path does not mean compromising our environmental goals but rather pursuing them with a clear-eyed understanding of the challenges and opportunities that lie ahead.

In this spirit, the time has come for an awakening—a realization that the stewardship of our planet requires not just passion and zeal but a grounded, informed approach that balances the environmental, economic, and social pillars of sustainability. By fostering a dialogue that is evidence-based, and open to critique, we can ensure that our march towards a more sustainable future does not lose sight of the forest for the trees.

Indeed, as we draw inspiration from historical analogies like the battle-hardened unity of the 1976 Canadiens, let us remember that the strength to confront and overcome challenges lies in our ability to unite in pursuit of common goals. An approach is needed-one that navigates the delicate balance between idealistic aspirations and the pragmatic realities of our world. In doing so, we not only honor the legacy of those who have navigated tumultuous times before us but also lay the groundwork for a future where environmental stewardship and societal well-being go hand in hand.

A New Path Forward

As we conclude our enlightening journey through the whimsical yet insightful land of Unicornia, it's clear that the realms of imagination have much to teach us about the realities of our world. Unicornia, with its exaggerated reflections of our society, has served not just as an escape but as a mirror, highlighting the critical areas where we must dare to envision change.

Our exploration has underscored the urgent need to dismantle the prevailing DEI framework, which, despite its noble intentions, often divides more than it unites. It is time to champion a new paradigm—Meritocracy, Innovation, and Equality (MIE). MIE advocates for a society where individuals are recognized and rewarded based on their merits, where innovation is encouraged across all sectors, and where equality is truly about giving everyone a fair chance to succeed.

Throughout the chapters, we've also delved into the specific challenges that men face in contemporary society—a narrative often silenced amidst loud discourses. The struggles and strengths of men, particularly in educational and social contexts, have been laid bare, not to compete with other narratives but to complete the mosaic of human experience.

Our journey through Unicornia has equally questioned the prevailing climate dogma, challenging the simplicity of utopian environmental solutions that often overlook the complex trade-offs required in real-world stewardship. By adopting a stance that values dialogue over dictation and pragmatism over panic, we invite a critique of policies and practices that might exacerbate the problems they aim to solve or impose undue burdens on the disadvantaged.

In reconnecting with these fundamentals, we pave the way for a more balanced, thoughtful, and productive society. One where the lessons from Unicornia are not just fantastical musings but actionable insights. A society that values the contributions of all its members and recognizes the unique challenges they face.

As we step out of the kaleidoscopic gates of Unicornia, let us carry with us the resolve to make these necessary changes. Let our journey be a catalyst for conversation and action, inspiring others to join us in reshaping our world. The path may be fraught with challenges, but the destination—a world that upholds MIE, values true education, and recognizes every individual's struggle and strength—is worth every effort.

"Critical Queries for the Climate Conundrum"

This appendix gathers a series of pivotal inquiries aimed at unraveling the complexities and confronting the contradictions within the current climate discourse. These questions are essential for fostering a balanced and informed dialogue on environmental policies and their broader implications:

Evaluating the Toll of Net Zero: What repercussions will the pursuit of net zero emissions have on the globe's most disadvantaged populations? Is there a risk that this endeavor could lead to a reduction in living standards for a substantial number of people?

Clarifying 'Net Zero': Could you provide a precise explanation of the 'Net Zero' concept? What does achieving net zero emissions entail, and how is it defined within the context of current environmental policies?

Survival Without Fossil Fuels: How are individuals residing in extreme northern climates, such as the Arctic regions of Canada and Siberia, expected to sustain their communities in the absence of fossil fuel-based energy?

Carbon Taxes and Economic Vulnerability: What are the anticipated consequences of implementing carbon taxes on economically vulnerable and impoverished groups?

The Electric Vehicle Paradox: Echoing a point raised by Mr. Toyoda, how is the shift towards electric vehicles rationalized in a world where a significant portion of the population lacks access to basic electrical services?

Addressing All Major Polluters: While environmental advocacy often highlights the pollution contributions of specific industries, why is there a noticeable silence on the environmental impacts of the American Military Industrial Complex and China's rapid industrial expansion?

The Davos Dilemma: For those who champion carbon reduction yet continue to attend elite gatherings via private jet, how do you reconcile your personal carbon footprint with the message of emission reduction preached to the general populace?

Mitigating Climate Anxiety Among Youth: What strategies are in place to mitigate the growing mental health concerns among children and adolescents induced by climate change alarmism?

Falsifiability of 'Climate Change': Is the concept of climate change structured in a way that allows for empirical testing and falsification? If so, what mechanisms are in place to facilitate this?

Transparency in Climate Modeling: What specific models are informing the current climate agenda, and how transparent are these models in terms of their data, methodologies, and predictions?

LINKS TO CLIMATE CHANGE PREDICTION

1. 1967: Dire Famine Forecast By 1975. https://shorturl
.at/n7C6a

2. 1969: Everyone Will Disappear In a Cloud Of Blue
Steam By 1989 (1969) https://shorturl.at/9IT3G

3. 1970: Ice Age By 2000. https://shorturl.at/pT5tT

4. 1970: America Subject to Water Rationing By 1974 and
Food Rationing By 1980. https://shorturl.at/QGcoH

5. 1971: New Ice Age Coming By 2020 or 2030 https://s
horturl.at/2tAsZ

6. 1972: New Ice Age By
2070 https://www.cpc.ncep.noaa.gov/products/ou
treach/CDPW40/CD&PW_reeves_denver.pdf

7. 1974: Space Satellites Show New Ice Age Coming
Fast https://www.newspapers.com/image/259696
938/?terms=new+ice+age

8. 1974: Another Ice Age?
web.archive.org/web/20060812025725/http:/time
-proxy.yaga.com/time/archive/printout/0,23657,94
4914,00.html

9. 1974: Ozone Depletion a 'Great Peril to Life (data and graph) https://www.newspapers.com/image/6965 1456/?terms=ozon+depletion

10. 1976: Scientific Consensus Planet Cooling, Famines imminent https://www.nytimes.com/1976/07/18/archiv es/the-genesis-strategy-a-chilling-prospect.html

11. 1980: Acid Rain Kills Life In Lakes (additional link) https://www.newspapers.com/image/353862 247/?terms=%22acid+rain%22+and+kill+before

12. 1978: No End in Sight to 30-Year Cooling Trend (additional link) https://timesmachine.nytimes.com/tim esmachine/1978/01/05/issue.html

13. 1988: Regional Droughts (that never happened) in 1990s https://realclimatescience.com/2019/05/hansen-g ot-everything-wrong-alarmists-claim-victory/

14. 1988: Temperatures in DC Will Hit Record Highs https://realclimatescience.com/2019/05/hansen-g ot-everything-wrong-alarmists-claim-victory/

15. 1988: Maldive Islands will Be Underwater by 2018 (they're not) trove.nla.gov.au/newspaper/article/10 2074798

16. 1989: Rising Sea Levels will Obliterate Nations if Nothing Done by 2000 https://www.newspapers.com/image/247922

164/?terms=global+warming+noel+brown

17. 1989: New York City's West Side Highway Underwater by 2019 (it's not) https://wayback.archive.org/web/20110202162233/ https:/www.salon.com/books/int/2001/10/23/we ather/

18. 2000: Children Won't Know what Snow Is https://web.archive.org/web/20150912124604/http :/www.independent.co.uk/environment/snowfalls -are-now-just-a-thing-of-the-past-724017.html

19. 2002: Famine In 10 Years If We Don't Give Up Eating Fish, Meat, and Dairy https://www.theguardian.com /environment/2004/feb/22/usnews.theobserver

20. 2004: Britain will Be Siberia by 2024 https://www.theguardian.com/environment/ 2004/feb/22/usnews.theobserver

21. 2008: Arctic will Be Ice Free by 2018 https://news.google.com/newspapers?nid=1988&da t=20080624&id=7mgiAAAAIBAJ&sjid=7qkFAAAAIBAJ &pg=5563,4123490

22. 2008: Climate Genius Al Gore Predicts Ice-Free Arctic by 2013 https://wattsupwiththat.com/2018/12/16/ten-year s-ago-algore-predicted-the-north-polar-ice-cap-w ould-be-gone-inconveniently-its-still-there/

23. 2009: Climate Genius Prince Charles Says we Have

96   Months   to   Save   World
https://www.independent.co.uk/environment/gree
n-living/just-96-months-to-save-world-says-princ
e-charles-1738049.html

24. 2009: UK Prime Minister Says 50 Days to 'Save The
Planet   From   Catastrophe'
content.usatoday.com/communities/ondeadline/p
ost/2009/12/gore-new-study-sees-nearly-ice-free
-arctic-summer-ice-cap-as-early-as-2014/1#.XVm
6Py2ZNu3

25. 2009: Climate Genius Al Gore Moves 2013 Prediction
of   Ice-Free   Arctic   to   2014
https://www.theguardian.com/environment/earth
-insight/2013/jul/24/arctic-ice-free-methane-eco
nomy-catastrophe

26. 2013: Arctic Ice-Free by 2015 (additional link)
https://www.theguardian.com/environment/earth
-insight/2013/jul/24/arctic-ice-free-methane-eco
nomy-catastrophe

27. 2014: Only 500 Days Before 'Climate Chaos'
https://www.washingtonexaminer.com/weekly-sta
ndard/planet-still-standing-500-days-after-french
-foreign-minister-warned-of-climate-chaos

28. 1968: Overpopulation Will Spread Worldwide
https://www.smithsonianmag.com/innovation/boo
k-incited-worldwide-fear-overpopulation-18096749
9/

29. 1970: World Will Use Up All its Natural Resources www.mining.com/the-world-is-not-running-out-of-natural-resources/

30. 2006: Super Hurricanes! https://www.breitbart.com/the-media/2015/06/01/media-fail-no-major-hurricanes-in-9-years/

31. 2005 : Manhattan Underwater by 2015 https://www.newsbusters.org/blogs/scott-whitlock/2015/06/12/flashback-abcs-08-prediction-nyc-under-water-climate-change-june

32. 18 spectacularly wrong predictions made around the time of first Earth Day in 1970, expect more this year | American Enterprise Institute - AEI

www.ingramcontent.com/pod-product-compliance
Lightning Source LLC
Chambersburg PA
CBHW052132270326
41930CB00012B/2856